A STARFISH AT A TIME

How Our Family of 19 Grew Through Adoption

Dana Wynn Steele

Carpenter's Son Publishing

A Starfish at a Time: How Our Family of 19 Grew Through Adoption

©2013 by Dana Wynn Steele

Published by Carpenter's Son Publishing, Franklin, Tennessee

Published in association with
Larry Carpenter of Christian Book Services, LLC
www.christianbookservices.com

Unless otherwise noted, Scripture is taken from the HOLY BIBLE, NEW INTERNATIONAL VERSION®. Copyright © 1973, 1978, 1984 Biblica. Used by permission of Zondervan. All rights reserved.

Cover Painting by Margi Wynn

Cover and Interior Design by Suzanne Lawing

Editing by Robert Irvin

Printed in the United States of America

978-1-940262-05-5

WHAT PEOPLE ARE SAYING

"The number of orphaned and vulnerable children needing families in this country is staggering. Dana Wynn Steele and her husband, Alan, understand the need and the challenges involved in making a difference. I have been in their home, met their children, and watched them love their kids. It's all about family - being there for each other, giving each other space to heal, and believing in the value of each and every person. Easy words on paper -- much more difficult to walk out.

We all need to read this book in order to understand the children who are waiting, the system they are "stuck" in, and the opportunity we all have to make a difference.

Pray for this courageous couple and then ask God how He wants to use you. Not everyone is called to adopt or foster, but we are all called to do something... one starfish at a time!"

Terry Meeuwsen
Co-host, The 700 Club
Founder, Orphan's Promise

"If you are a Servant Leader; have faith that when you pray to God, He will listen-and, more importantly answer; subscribe to Golden Rule Behavior; possess an equalitarian spirit for all, a profound love of people and a desire to make a positive contribution to society, than this book is a must read for you. Dana's story will inspire you and fill you with hope; and, if you share my sentimentality, you also might shed a tear or two. Of one thing, I am certain: by the time you read the last page in this touching story, you will realize that while you may have shared your clowing Servant's Heart with others, if you want to follow Dana and Alan's lead, then you have many, many miles to go before you sleep."

Colleen Barrett
President Emeritus, Southwest Airlines
Co-Author of the book, Lead with LUV, A Different Way to Create Real Success

An old man was walking on the beach one morning when he came across an area where hundreds of live starfish had been washed onto the sand. A little boy was running up and down the beach picking up the starfish one by one and throwing them back into the waves as far as he could. The old man went up to the boy and said, "Son, it's impossible for you to get all of these starfish into the ocean; there are too many. You won't be able to make a difference by yourself." The boy scooped up the next starfish, threw it into the sea, and said, "It made a difference to that one! And that one!" as he continued throwing them back into the sea.

DEDICATION

This book is dedicated to the greatest gift God has given me after His salvation for me: my husband, Alan K. Steele. Alan is a loving and terrific husband, and a dedicated, patient father. God has truly blessed me with a man who has the desire to listen to Him and be obedient. Even though he jokingly tells others that he lines the kids up in the morning, counts them, and then counts them again in the evening to make sure I haven't slipped any in without him noticing, he never says no to a child in need that God calls us to welcome into our family. I'm so thankful to God that He has blessed me with a man willing to serve Him.

AUTHOR'S NOTE

Our system of foster care, while helping children to get out of unsafe home environments, needs help. God calls us, as the Church, to make a difference in the lives of orphans and the fatherless. (See Exodus 22:22-24; Deut 10:18 and 24:17; Psalm 82:3; James 1:27, to name a few). But what does that mean in our individual lives as we seek to obey God?

There are a few churches that have taken up the cause of the fatherless and have developed foster care "agencies" through their body of believers (Calvary Chapel Fort Lauderdale's 4Kids program is a good example). There are others who have taken God's command to heart and have adopted children through foster care, as a body, such as Bennett Chapel in Possum Trot, Texas. These are all needs, and necessary through God's Word to show His love for the fatherless, as the apostle James writes. But what does God require of us personally?

Anyone can hear God's call for the fatherless and respond. Adoption in the United States through foster care takes commitment, but the rewards are much more abundant than the commitment itself. Adoptive parents can be single, older, or even newly married. There is usually a monthly stipend to help in the expenses for the children and often medical care is available as well. All it requires is a few classes, and a heart willing to make the difference in the life of a child. Every child deserves a family of their own.

Perhaps you or your family are unable to adopt or to foster children. However, you can help those who are called in this ministry. You can offer to babysit; to give respite for adoptive parents who just need a break, particularly if they have a large family; give school clothes or school supplies to help ease the financial burden; or even just be a shoulder to cry on when an adoptive parent has reached their limit. God can use every one of us to heed his call to care for the fatherless.

Remember the heroes of the Bible who were adopted, including Moses, and Jesus, who was adopted by his earthly father, Joseph. Remember that we are all adopted sons and daughters into the family of God. And to quote my friend from NASA, Dr. Terry Morris, remember that "the least of these," as described in Matthew 25:31-46, are the homeless and the fatherless.

OUR FIRST SURPRISE

The call came about 10 AM as I stared out onto the snow covering our lawn in Chesapeake, Virginia. We had arrived home late the previous evening from a week in San Diego. I missed warm Southern California as the car stopped in front of a pile of snow in our front yard.

"Hi Dana, I have a special request for you. It's a baby boy, and he has some injuries, but we think he's fine now." Mary P., from Social Services, was calling asking us to take in a baby that had most probably been injured in his parent's care, and was now in the care of the State of Virginia. He was in the hospital, ready to be released;

only there was no home for him. Mary continued, "We know you all already have a brain-injured baby, and this little boy has been shaken, but hasn't suffered any lasting effects. He's fine. Well, except for the thirty-six broken bones. He is only three months old, and we don't have anyone else…. Please, will you take him?"

I mumbled something about Alan, then quickly called him at the restaurant we owned. "Honey, I know we agreed that we were content with just adopting girls, but Mary has just called. It's a three-month-old boy. Thirty-six broken bones. What do you think?" Alan told me later that he was stunned. He stammered, "You will need to go to the hospital, speak with the doctors, and figure out if we can handle this. What about Hailee?"

Hailee was our blonde, blue-eyed, ten-month-old little girl brought to us from Social Services with Shaken Baby Syndrome. She was finally sitting up, crawling, and eating some on her own, after much therapy. She had cerebral palsy from the shaking that occurred when she was five weeks old. We had picked her up from the same Children's Hospital a week later. Her caseworker had already chosen us stating, "You will adopt her."

We were all exhausted. When our eighteen-year-old daughter Kara had come home from her two-month trip to Europe visiting relatives in December, we headed back to San Diego. We'd moved to Virginia just eighteen months ago.

Kara and Aimee, our four-year-old, had both been born in San Diego. Alan's family still lived there; so we had gone back just after Christmas with Kara, Hailee, and Aimee, who had been adopted years before from

San Diego Social Services. A trip to celebrate a late Christmas, introduce our family and friends to Hailee, and reconnect with old friends. We hadn't even unpacked yet, and Kara was still asleep. I woke her quickly. "I'm heading to the hospital. Please watch Hailee and Aimee."

As I walked into the Children's Hospital, I was nervous about what I would see when I reached the bed where this little boy was. I could see the injured and sick children all around me, and smelled the fumes of cleaning fluid in the air, as well as the fried cafeteria food. My first stop was to meet with Sandy, the hospital social worker. "I remember you… when you picked up Hailee." She smiled. "Thank you for being willing to explore taking this little boy home." She eagerly reached for my hand, her expression hopeful and welcoming to me. She was shorter than I (which is quite short, as I'm only 5'4") but exuded confidence as she started to walk quickly ahead of me.

"I've come to find out more so my husband and I can decide." Sandy smiled again. "You are this child's new parents," she excitedly told me. "I'm so thankful it is you instead of the foster mom who was here yesterday. She decided the baby was too fussy, and you should have seen her long fingernails."

I spoke with Sandy as well as the attending physician and all of the nurses in charge of the baby boy; they all confirmed his happy disposition. "He's not fussy at all," they chorused. One shared, "He is in pain,but the medication seems to be helping." He does not seem to be showing any aftereffects from the shaking. His pain was from skull fractures; he had two, on either side of his head, sort of like a cracked egg shell."

His broken bones were in different stages of healing. His most recent fractures were his ribs, which had been broken twice, and were now fractured in the back. "He needs to sleep on his stomach."

While it sounded daunting, he did not have any casts, and the doctor assured me his other fractures were mostly healed. The main ones, radial fractures (the twisting kind), were on his left arm, his lower left leg, and his upper right thigh. The nurses on duty continued to assure me, He has a most pleasant, sunny disposition. We're astounded that the foster mother refused taking him for being "fussy." Sandy, the hospital social worker, shared "His responses are normal and there is no indication of brain injury that would occur from shaking. Unlike Hailee."

Because family members had initially brought the baby to the hospital, and his injuries were determined to be purposely inflicted, the hospital staff had given him an alias. "He is Jack Frost now." This was primarily to prevent the family from having contact until it could be determined exactly how he was injured, and by whom. Hospital X-rays and records confirmed that he had his first bone broken at just under one month old, and his collarbone in two places. The medical staff were unable to determine how or when the other bones had been broken, only that they had occurred over the subsequent two months after the broken collarbone.

I went into the room to see the baby Jack Frost. It was a large, sterile place with a baby-sized hospital bed, and all kinds of machines surrounding it. The baby was this tiny-looking guy stuck in the middle of this seemingly monstrous bed. He looked at me as I walked in, and smiled, his big brown eyes lighting up. He had hair like Don King, the loud and famous boxing promoter of the 70s and 80s, sticking straight up, medium-brown skin, and was only wearing a diaper and a onesie. As I bent over to take his hand, God seemed to be speaking to me directly, and I felt immediately, "*This is my son.*" Whatever misgivings I had before disappeared at that moment. But how could I convince Alan?

The hospital staff weren't ready to release baby Jack, so I left without promising them anything. On the way home, I called Alan. I began crying, "Alan, this is our son. God told me that he's ours." Without any hesitation, he responded, "OK, contact Mary at Social Services, and the hospital, and we'll pick him up as soon as he's ready to leave. I'll go with you."

Relief flooded me as I made the phone calls, and then began running around with our younger girls in tow, trying to locate a crib and some clothes to get by with. I knew he would be released from the hospital only in a diaper and a blanket. Thankfully, through our local adoption and foster care community, I gathered a crib, new bottles, and a couple of blankets and onesies before we headed for the hospital that evening.

When we first walked into baby Jack's hospital room, I held my breath to see Alan's first reaction. I needn't have worried. Alan walked right up to the hospital bed and the baby started laughing at him; Alan engaged him right away. He turned to the nurse. "Can I pick him up and hold him?" She nodded, and father and son began giggling and laughing together. I'm sorry to this day that I didn't record it, but I will remember it forever. They truly bonded instantly. As I predicted, we left with the baby clad in a T-shirt and diaper, wrapped in a hospital blanket, with extra diapers and formula. A whole new chapter in our lives had started, and a whole new life for baby Jack Frost.

BACK TO THE BEGINNING

How did ordinary, working professionals like us end up with so many children, and special needs kids at that? Our family's story started much earlier, in San Diego. At the time Alan and I married, he was a single dad to three children: Brendan 14, Kevin 11, and Kara, 7. Although he and his former wife shared custody, just after we married, Kevin came to live with us full time. I was a flight attendant for Southwest Airlines, and had just finished law school; Alan owned a market, a Seven Eleven franchise, and a deli, all within a two-mile radius in the San Diego community of Clairemont. I opened my law practice within a few months of our wedding.

As our lives together began, I mentioned to Alan, "I would like us to consider adoption", I was unable to have children. He told me that he was against it, as his kids (now ours) needed too much time and attention. I dropped the subject, as the children we already had needed a lot from both of us. We set about together parenting them, and I began building my law practice, flying for Southwest on weekends until, as an attorney, I was able to help pay the bills.

Six years later, I found out about a surgery that would allow me to conceive. I asked Alan, "Can we consider this?" He told me, "Look into it Dana, but I'm reluctant to have any more children."

So I began praying, asking my prayer group to pray with me that God would change Alan's heart. All the while I never raised the question with him again. Almost a year to the day after we all began praying, Alan gave me a card he had picked out for me while we were on a vacation in Hawaii; the card announced that he was ready to have another child with me. God had truly worked a miracle in changing his heart, and even more of a miracle in teaching me to keep my mouth shut. We discussed the operation versus adoption, and together made the decision to adopt. It was the best and most surprising vacation I've ever had!

As a lawyer working with cases involving Social Services, I was well aware that there were many children available for adoption in San Diego County. We signed up with Angels, a foster care agency that had contracted with the county to take care of children under three. We began preparing for a new baby, excited for a new addition to our family. I had a wonderful time with shopping, choosing an antique crib and matching bassinet at my favorite antique shop, and decorating one of our bedrooms with blue and white Victorian wallpaper and matching paint. I desperately wanted to rush out and buy baby clothes and diapers, but of course, we had no idea when we'd get the child or what size our new little one would be. Such is the difference in preparation for adoption than the nine months of waiting for a newborn! Our church friends helped, decorating the crib and making teddy bears to match the wallpaper. They were as excited as we were for us to welcome a new little one into our lives.

How to prepare our parents? My parents were getting used to "surprises" from me in my life with Alan. For instance, when we were engaged, we planned our wedding for a weekend in May when my family would be sure to be able to attend, centering it around my law school graduation. However, we had purchased a house in February of the same year, and eloped so that we wouldn't have to pay for two residences in anticipation of our upcoming marriage. I called my parents the night before our wedding on Valentine's Day: "Change of plans Mom and Dad!" We still had plans for our May wedding. And Alan's parents had figured it out because they helped move the contents of my home at the beach four blocks over to our newly purchased home the weekend before our elopement.

I grew up in Northern Virginia, near Washington, D.C. in a Christian home, accepting Jesus as my Lord and Savior when I was twelve years old. My mother was a stay-at-home mom, Bible study leader, and prayer counselor. She later acquired a Masters' Degree in Christian counseling. My father had worked at various computer and Christian companies over the years, most recently for Regent University in Virginia Beach.

Alan was born in San Diego but had grown up first in Virginia Beach and then back in San Diego; his parents had moved back and forth from one coast to the other, first when Alan was a toddler, and then again when he was fourteen, as his dad was transferred with the Navy. Alan had given his life to the Lord when he was thirty-five, just after we started dating. His dad had since been retired from the Navy and had owned a very profitable Seven Eleven franchise for about twenty years; his parents were still living in San Diego just a couple of miles from our home. We were therefore able to prepare them personally for our news about our upcoming addition to our family. We took them out to their favorite Italian place for dinner. I was so nervous to let them know that I barely ate my dinner, highly unusual for me! "We are getting ready to adopt a baby girl, and it's highly likely the child will not be Caucasian." We wanted our families to be ready for any child that God chose to give us. Alan's parents were gracious and excited; so were mine when we called them the same weekend.

Parents have to take classes if they are going to adopt through social services or any agency that helps social service agencies. The classes give an overview of the many special needs the potential children may have. In the introductory class, when asked if we would accept special needs children, we immediately said no, thinking we were ill equipped to handle a child in a wheelchair or a blind child. We discovered that the term "special needs" often means little more than a child not of Caucasian race, a child over four years old, or members of a sibling group. Additionally, 90 percent of San Diego County's children are in foster care or ready for adoption due to drugs—either they were exposed to drugs, addicted (as babies), or their parents have some connection with drugs. The special needs label for these children has to do with the drugs they have been exposed to or harmed by.

Meanwhile, the agency called. "We might have a fifteen-month old girl to place. Interested?" We were startled, as we expected an infant, but said, "We'll consider taking her, if she comes into your agency, and if another infant does not come in first." We didn't hear anything more about this little girl.

A month passed, and we got another call from the agency. The toddler girl, Aimee, was available, and we needed to pick her up immediately from a temporary foster home. We walked into a tiny, crowded two bedroom apartment, with a napping baby in a crib in the living room, and a three-year-old crying on the foster mom's lap. As we sat down, Aimee toddled out of the bedroom from a nap. Alan got down on his knees, and she walked right into his arms. He looked up at me with tears in his eyes, and said, "Wow, she looks just like me!"

Aimee was a joy from the first day. With her curly dark hair and dark eyes, she did resemble Alan a little. Since she was biracial, her slightly darker skin tone made her look exotic; we were often asked if she were Hawaiian or Puerto Rican. She had just recently learned to walk, so she was hesitant on her feet, often walking into walls or doors as she hurried down the hall to the next terrorizing of our family dogs. She was developmentally delayed and we discovered almost immediately that she had been exposed to drugs, methamphetaminc, during most of her nine months in the womb. Her birth mother, Crystal, lived with her a short time after her birth, manufacturing methamphetamine in the home, and even leaving the drug paraphernalia in Aimee's crib. They lived with Crystal's sometimes boyfriend, Jimmy, and his mother, Sharon. Crystal did not do the day-to-day care for Aimee; she would often walk by her without stopping when Aimee was crying to be fed or have her diaper changed. Sharon cared for Aimee from the beginning of her life, arranging for her child care during her working hours at the local children's shelter. Crystal disappeared when Aimee was around five months old, and had never been heard from again.

Sharon was insistent that Aimee was her granddaughter. Although I think she knew in her heart that her son Jimmy was not Aimee's father, she was reluctant to give her up. She couldn't raise her because of a background that included a criminal past (distant past), and allegations that her son had molested children she had been fostering several years before. San Diego Social Services was unable to take any risks with Aimee. Sharon asked: "Pull up Aimee's shirt. See how light-skinned she is?" Further "proof" that she was related to Sharon. The social workers were not impressed, but allowed her one or two supervised visits per month at a local Mc-Donald's restaurant, the typical visiting place for any children and their birth family members in most parts of the country.

I felt sorry for Sharon, but her son Jimmy was adamant that Crystal was already pregnant when he met her. He was not the father, he said, adding that he had been advised not to take a paternity test. Crystal had named a Steven Bishop as the father when she first applied for welfare and food stamps. I asked Sharon, "Can you persuade Jimmy to take the paternity test?" She said, "He refuses."

Jimmy, his father, and Sharon were all Caucasian, as were Crystal and her birthparents. Aimee was clearly the child of a mixed liason. I gently explained to Sharon that the odds of Jimmy being the father, based upon the timing of his meeting and dating Crystal as well as the race of the parents and grandparents, was practically zero. The social workers did find a Steven Bishop through California social security records. He lived in Northern California and insisted that he had never been to San Diego and did not know Crystal. Steven took the paternity test. He was not her father.

California had just passed a law the year before. Birth parents had only six months to comply with court orders in order to reunify with children under the age of three, although a judge had discretion to give more time if progress was made. The clock is supposed to start ticking when the child comes under the protection of Social Services. In reality, it usually starts about a month or more later, once the case is first brought to court.

Since Aimee's birth mom was nowhere to be found, and all that was known about her birth dad was a possible name of Steven Bishop, and that he was African-American, the social workers assumed that we would be adopting her quickly after seven months. In the meantime, we found out all that we could about the way in utero drug exposure affected her. She began therapy for speech and developmental delays in the months that followed. A therapist came into our home several times a week to work on Aimee's learning delays, showing her how to do things with blocks, puzzles, and moving her legs with her. The speech therapist worked with her on making sounds, but Aimee was still unable to make the sounds into words. She had one word that she said over and over, which worked for "dog," "Daddy," and anything she was excited about, and sounded like "dagnun."

Just three weeks before the court hearing that would release Aimee for the adoption, a call came from the social worker. Crystal had materialized and wanted custody. As an attorney I was fairly certain that after abandoning her child for so long (17 months), the judge wasn't going to change custody. Yet I knew that proceedings could now drag out indefinitely. We gathered a lot of photographs of Aimee so that Crystal could see how she had changed over the last year and a half from an infant to a 20-month-old toddler with a personality of her own. We met her for the first time at what was supposed to be the last hearing before the adoption began.

Crystal immediately looked at the pictures and greeted us warmly as we introduced ourselves. "I know

I have little chance of getting Aimee back, but I want you to adopt her if I can't." The judge only gave her one extra month, although it actually stretched out into three months. During this time, she visited with Aimee and I at the Angel's agency several times, drug tested for her social worker, and had a complete psychological evaluation done. The evaluation results were not positive, although Crystal had not been using drugs for several months. The bottom line of the evaluator's report stated that Crystal, herself abandoned by first her own mother, then her father, was repeating the same cycle. She would most likely abandon any other child if given the opportunity. Additionally, she was just barely surviving, and was living with another boyfriend and his family, working part-time in a fast food restaurant, her first job. She simply was not capable of parenting a child, much less one with special needs. The judge ultimately terminated her parental rights.

We adopted Aimee several months later. We celebrated with a big adoption party as well as her baby dedication the same weekend that our Army son, Kevin, came home from Kuwait. My entire family flew out from Virginia.

We tried to continue a relationship with Crystal, and a separate one with Sharon. Crystal would make plans to meet us somewhere and never show up. I believe she wanted to see Aimee, but it was too difficult, logistically and emotionally. Sharon faithfully visited Aimee at a local McDonald's every month until we relocated to the East Coast. We continued to call and correspond with Sharon, but Crystal had dropped out of sight. All of our recent attempts to locate her have been unsuccessful.

In spite of our inability to provide a continued relationship between Aimee and her birth mom, she has grown into a lovely young lady, playing sports for her school, and now on a travel soccer team. The after effects of her drug exposure are seen in what has been termed by her neurologist as a brain injury. This affects her learning, but Aimee is doing well at her school with specialized tutoring. She is a loving child with a warm heart for God, for missions, and for evangelism.

Aimee (age 14) says today: *Being adopted was the best thing that ever happened to me, because I'm in a really fun and active family. I'm glad that I know Jesus and that I've learned about Him through my family. I'm glad I can be active in sports and have lots of friends through private school, church, and American Heritage Girls. I would not have had these friends and opportunities if I didn't have this family.*

MOVING MIRACLE

Just a month after Aimee's adoption, my grandmother passed away in Virginia, and we all headed back East for the funeral. As soon as we returned, Alan surprised me. "How do you feel if we move from San Diego, possibly back to Virginia?"

Almost all of his family lived in San Diego; he had lived there for thirty years, and I had been there for seventeen. Our careers, friends, church, and home were there; yet I was tempted to think about living somewhere less expensive than California, where I could stay home more with the children and live closer to my family. My parents and sisters all lived within ten miles of each other, and I had nephews that we only saw once a year. We prayed about it over the weekend.

We never mentioned this to anyone. On Monday following this conversation, a man came into our deli asking for Alan. "I'm interested in purchasing your market, the one about a mile down this street." We were stunned. No one had ever offered to purchase any of our businesses before. Not only did he want to buy the market, he offered us exactly what we would have listed it for with a business broker. We knew God was working in our lives, but weren't sure why.

The next day, one of the deli employees came to Alan with a strange request. "I want to be the first to be considered as a buyer for the deli, should you ever decide to sell." We were dumbfounded. We'd figured it would take us six months or longer to sell our businesses and our home. It seemed that God was ordering things quickly for us.

We called a Realtor to look at our house and list it for sale. Early in the morning of our appointment, our next door neighbor came over and asked, "Have you ever considered selling your home? If so, my best friend wants to buy it."

I told her we were meeting with our Realtor that afternoon, but she asked us to put it off until her friends could come over and speak to us. Later in the day, the friends came over and offered us exactly what we were going to list our house for. We were so amazed. In three days, we had sold both of our businesses and our home without mentioning a word. It was definitely the hand of God moving us to Virginia, though we were still unsure as to His plan for us. We were on our way to a new life and whatever God had for us next.

By the middle of August we were in our new home in Virginia: a four-bedroom with a pool in a neighborhood (as opposed to the country home we'd had in San Diego). My favorite parts were the sunken spa tub, the dressing room added onto the master bedroom, and loads of closet space! Alan was putting together the final touches for our new restaurant, Al's Diner, a 50s diner we opened near our home. We had a wonderful time hitting the antique stores and decorating with 50s themed memorabilia—a statue of Elvis; another one of Betty Boop; old records and our California license plates to decorate the walls. Our red and royal blue nagahide booths, large jukebox, and a black and white tiled floor made it look like a real soda shop and diner.

I concentrated those first few months in our new home getting Aimee, then three, and Kara, 17, settled into their new schools. How would they cope? Kara starting a new school and a new life as a senior, and Aimee, with her mostly unintelligible speech, in a new home and new preschool?

Aimee began preschool at Virginia Beach Preschool of the Arts, which concentrated on music and dance. We soon found that she needed a more structured pre-academic environment to help with her speech and physical delays. We moved her to another preschool closer to our home and to Kara's new school. While it was a better fit, it was a much stricter environment, and even as a preschooler, required more from her than she was capable of at three years of age. I was soon spending time at the school and in the principal's office, although I had to continually remind myself, and the school staff, "She is only three!"

Meanwhile, we had gone through the process to become foster parents again (it must be repeated in each state) and were blessed with the arrival of Hailee into our home in March of 2003. Hailee was six weeks old, and had been shaken sometime between her fourth and fifth week of life. Although her prognosis was good, she started in therapy almost immediately to help with anticipated delays in movement. Her birth mom had already given up Hailee's older brother to relatives, and it seemed highly unlikely that she could handle another child with brain injuries.

One thing we have learned through our years fostering and adopting with different public social service agencies is this: if your child needs therapy at any age, it is up to you, the foster/adoptive parents, to seek it out and obtain it for your child. This can be daunting, particularly if you are new in the area and have no idea who to contact to begin therapy. While therapeutic services are briefly mentioned in foster care and adoptive training, there are no specifics given as to what agencies to contact, how to get therapy for your child, and what agencies will do assessments.

And unfortunately, *none* of the social service agencies that we have worked with insist on foster parents taking their children to therapy. When a child is placed in the next foster home available, no one asks if the parents can afford therapy. The prevailing thought is that foster parents provide food, clothing, and a roof over the child. Therapy, regardless of how much it's needed, is considered an added bonus. I know of numerous foster parents who are adequate caregivers but do not have their children participate in any kind of therapy. I have always had an internal struggle for I have often seen children who could have progressed so much more rapidly if they had been able to have therapy.

Hailee was a joy in our home, although it involved work, keeping up with her therapies as well as Aimee's. Hailee's cerebral palsy, the kind with loose muscle tone (as opposed to the kind with tight muscles), affected all of her motor skills, required to do simple things like holding a bottle or eating. It also affected her ability to hold her head up early on, and later, to sit up, to pull up, and eventually to walk.

We were given the name and number of Hailee's pediatrician, who had been seeing her since her birth. Dr. Barnwell confirmed, "Prior to her brain injuries, Hailee was holding her head up and completing all of her milestones as a newborn and young infant." Now she could no longer hold her head up and had a difficult time tracking objects with her eye movements. Dr. Barnwell and her partner in the pediatric office were amazing in keeping up with us and with Hailee. They called our home every night to check on her and helped us with any questions we had in monitoring her progress and watching for possible seizures related to her brain injuries.

Hailee's social worker visited our home after about seven months. "You can adopt her, as she is not likely to go back to the birth mother, and I don't think the grandparents want her either." Great news for us, as we were ready to adopt again. However, when Hailee was about 16 months, the social worker changed her mind after a disagreement with us over her therapy, and contacted the grandparents. They were surprised to hear from the social worker, as they were unwilling to even acknowledge a possible blood relationship after finding out about her brain injury. After we had worked with Hailee for so long through therapy and our own hard work, she had made enough progress that the grandparents were now quite willing to step in.

The other social workers in the agency were appalled; Hailee was thoroughly attached to our family, we were progressing well with her, and her grandparents in Indiana lived in a trailer miles away from any pediatric treatment facility. Nonetheless, the worker was able to manipulate the system so that the grandparents arrived on the day the case was to be litigated in court. She was able to plea to the judge, "They have driven over twelve hours to pick Hailee up, therefore there is no need to continue with the court case." We couldn't believe that after all this time, and all of the court hearings, the judge was not even going to listen to our lawyer and hear the case, but simply deferred to one social worker's opinion, without even hearing the facts.Our lawyer was devastated, as we were. I attempted to meet with the director of the social service agency, but she was bent on defending her worker who had lied to us, to her, and had made a poor decision for Hailee. I appeared to be just another hysterical foster parent who didn't know "my place" as it was later described, although I kept my cool and tried not to be emotional until the end of the meeting, when I realized no one was listening to me. The social worker came to our home to pick up Hailee, passing her around for each member of our family gathered there to say good-bye. Alan couldn't even see her; he had to go outside by himself and cry. The grandparents were able to leave immediately with Hailee, and to our family, it was as if she had died. It's still painful to relive that first night with her gone. Aimee kept asking where Hailee was, and when she was coming back. We had no answers for her, we couldn't even talk about it to each other. I've rarely seen Alan cry, and never this much—we both clung to each other and sobbed that night as we got into bed. We have never heard anything about her since, although we continue to contact the grandparents to ask for pictures and for an update.

While this is one of the most blatant examples of heartbreak connected with foster care, it happens. We are often told by people, "Oh, I could never do foster care and have to give the child back to someone else." All that I can say is that if God calls you to do something, you have to do it. God will handle whatever heartbreak results. I can't say that we'll ever forget Hailee, because it's like a child has been lost to death. God has healed up the hole in our hearts that was made with her departure, but we will never forget her.

I am constantly amazed at social services agencies when it comes to bonding and attachment. Our son Jake's worker told me that babies and toddlers, just like all of the kids in foster care, are expected to be able to attach, leave, and re-attach according to the agency's decisions. Whether it be another foster home, or relatives, or back with birth parents. I've seen children placed in foster care, then shifted back to their dysfunctional home, and shunted back into foster care again as the abuse in their natural home continues. I have seen children constantly moved from foster home to foster home, for no reason except that the social worker decides she doesn't like the foster parents anymore, or the foster parents decide they don't want to do foster care. We had two small children, an infant and a toddler, for six months, and they were moved for the simple reason that a different foster home was closer to the social service agency. The worker did not have to drive as far to pick them up for birth family visits.

For all of these children, the loss and grief is overwhelming, often resulting in delays in learning. Children get stuck at a certain age, unable to move on emotionally and sometimes academically. Yet the workers look at these children as files, almost as pieces of cardboard, rather than people who are experiencing loss every time they have to leave a home and try to re-attach with another family.

Alan and I decided long ago that we would not voluntarily give up any children in our care. Every child deserves to know that they are home for good, if they want to be. The only times children have left our home have been to live with their birth family, or because they chose not to be a part of our family (as in older teens). We made that commitment. Children who live with us can make this their permanent home.

BABY JAKE

So now we had two children under a year—our ten-month-old, Hailee, finally sitting up on her own, beginning to hold her own bottle, and eating baby food, and now Jack Frost. We were a bit unnerved. How could we help him with all of his injuries? We settled the baby that night attending to the huge list of instructions from the hospital for administering his pain medication. We lay awake discussing his name. "He looked more like a Jake, short for Jackson." "Yes, I agree. That suits him better." We were assuming that his real first name was Jack, and that the hospital staff had just given him a fake last name for safety. We were to learn later his first and last names, but by then, the name Jake had stuck.

Our girls were enamored with little Jake. He had a cheerful disposition as long as we kept up with his pain medication. Hailee, who was now crawling around the house, kept looking at him like she was expecting him to get off of the bed or out of the baby swing and crawl with her. Aimee wanted to help feed him, although she wasn't too excited about the diaper part. Kara was trying to decide if she wanted another brother; our oldest adult sons, Brendan and Kevin, lived out of state. Hailee had just recently begun to sleep through the night, allowing all of us those treasured seven to eight hours that I was now missing.

I took little Jake to our local pediatrician the next day after I faxed his hospital records to her office. Dr. Barnwell's careful fingers determined that in addition to all of his injuries, Jake was undernourished. "You'll need to wake him up several times during the night to feed him—strict regular feedings with a special formula." His little system couldn't handle the formula, so I asked Dr. Barnwell to change it. This changing continued for several months, because after about two weeks Jake couldn't keep the new formula in. We had to begin seeing a pediatric gastroenterologist (I didn't even know there was such a specialized doctor). Now, in addition to his own gastroenterologist, Jake had his own neurologist, neurosurgeon, orthopedic surgeon, physical therapist, ophthalmologist, and pediatrician. I got dizzy just trying to remember all of the names of the specialties, much less keeping track of all of his appointments.

We were shocked to discover from the gastroenterologist (tummy doctor, I called her) that once a baby has been shaken, all of his or her systems can be affected, sometimes for life. Jake's difficulty with keeping formula down appeared to be a direct result of the shaking. The brain injury affected his ability to digest his food. So we were caught in a two-to-three weeks cycle trying to get more expensive and difficult-to-obtain specialized formulas.

We soon noticed that Jake did not move like a normal four-month-old baby. He sat or lay stiffly with his head cocked to one side, and did not wave his arms or kick his legs when we played with him, changed him, or tickled him. Hailee's therapist Debbie, whom she saw every week, lived in our neighborhood. I asked if she could come over on a neighborly visit to take a look at Jake and see what we were seeing. We hoped she'd confirm that he was just a little delayed in his development. As Debbie watched his movements on the couch, on the floor, and in the swing, she looked concerned. "Jake needs to see the orthopedic surgeon before I can begin therapy. He looks like he has been in pain for a very long time."

The orthopedic doctor assured me that Jake could start therapy after his examination. We started with infant massage, moving his limbs so that he could begin to move normally on his own. Once the therapy started, Debbie and I began to see other alarming signs. Jake couldn't see anything on his right side. His apparent lack of sight, as well as his continued stiffness of movement on the right, was frightening. Something was still very wrong. Debbie contacted Dr. White, the original pediatric neurologist who had seen Jake in the emergency room the very first night he was brought in. Dr. White agreed to come with her to make a house call and examine Jake for himself, to possibly confirm what we were seeing.

After observing Jake and looking at the hospital records I had at home, Dr. White looked at us both and exclaimed, "Wait, I remember this baby. He was in so much pain and screaming so much when he was brought in that I had to have one of the volunteers hold him." He then looked at the MRI report from the scan done the night Jake was first taken to the hospital. He frowned. "This has been incorrectly interpreted. Jake was shaken twice within the same week, not just once, as was originally reported. Please make an appointment to get another CAT scan of his head, just to make sure that he's okay." He confirmed that there was a problem with his eyesight and his development. "This is related to the shaking."

As I was pulling out of the hospital parking lot after Jake's CAT scan, his pediatrician, who had been extremely helpful and solicitous the entire time we'd had Jake, called. "I've already received a copy of the scan. You need to make an immediate appointment with the Children's Hospital neurosurgeon." She wouldn't tell me much more, other than that Jake's scan looked abnormal. I tried to make an appointment, but the neurosurgeon's office had closed early that day, so I figured I would try again the next day.

The surgeon beat me to it. He called early the following morning and asked if Alan and I could both come to his office with Jake. Was he going to request additional tests? He surprised us. "Jake needs immediate brain surgery." He had developed water and fluid on his brain, a life-threatening condition. We were scheduled to leave the next morning for a special trip for foster parents to Orlando. We immediately cancelled it. We had to have Jake at the hospital early the next morning. We arrived early in the morning, and I felt so fortunate to have a compassionate nurse who was familiar with the surgeon. She told us that her daughter had a shunt put in by this same surgeon eighteen years before. I took the surgeon aside just before surgery to make sure he knew to shave Jake's entire head. He said, "I'm glad you told me, otherwise I would have just shaved the parts where we're doing the surgery." I thought it was much better for him to be bald for a couple of weeks and have his hair grow back evenly.

Jake's surgery was long and scary; we breathed a sigh of relief when the surgeon finished, and told us that shunting wasn't necessary. He was able to siphon the fluid from Jake's brain without any further trauma. We waited another hour for him to wake up in recovery, and I held his hand while he looked at Alan and I through the groggy haze of anesthesia. He emerged in ICU with a bandaged head and bright smile. I stayed with him every night, and he had a constant stream of visitors from our church family as well as my own extended family. He was bouncing back almost immediately, even with his head fully bandaged. He spent most of his time crawling around, looking for Hailee and grinning at us. Meanwhile, I was trying to stay with him as much as possible, running home to shower and change, check on the kids, and often bringing Hailee with me during the day so they could crawl around together. I would bring her back home at night so that I could sleep with him in his hospital room.

Alan and I both were able to get to know Jake's birth mom during his surgery. She was only allowed to visit Jake if Alan and I were there at the hospital; we were her official "supervisors" for visitation. I know now that God had it planned for us to be together so that we could begin to trust one another, as we will be tied together at least until Jake is eighteen, maybe even longer! I have learned to respect her and her loving decisions regarding Jake, and believe that she has come to respect both of us as well. Jake still visits with her at a local Mc-Donald's at least once or twice a year, and occasionally sees his birth sisters as well.

Jake began crawling around almost immediately, wanting to get on the floor and crawl with Hailee even at the hospital. He still had the cerebral palsy, which was manifest mostly in his fine motor skills, like hand movement and manipulation. He still has no vision from his nose all the way to the right, although his right eye works. Jake terms it "blind in one eye," although it's really blind on his right side. His gross motor skills are slightly affected; he still often trips and falls when he runs. After the surgery, he progressed to toddler stage by walking at about 10 to 11 months, normal for a baby's development.

We had been granted a miracle. God's timing was perfect. The neurologist had made a house call at just the right time. He had casually asked for another scan at exactly the right time. Our pediatrician, and the neurosurgeon, saw that scan. God knew what he was doing, just as He has planned Jake's life before Jake was even born. We often remind him of how much God loves him, and that God has a plan for his life.

Jake still sees his healing tribe—the neurologist, development specialist, ophthalmologist, his optometrist, and of course, his pediatrician, once a year. This entire community of health professionals works with us to ensure Jake remains on target for his development and his issues related to his brain injury. We've had to add a psychiatrist and two counselors so that he can work through the brain-processing challenges he has with academics as well as his everyday living skills.

Jake plays soccer, swims, rides horses, does karate, bikes, and skateboards. He is currently doing well in the small private Christian school. We monitor his academic progress closely since he has the potential for more brain dysfunction, given his health history. He knows that he is a lucky boy and that God spared his life for a reason, and he is a determined child, not prone to giving up easily on a task. Reading skills have proved to be harder for him to master, but he has finally turned a corner and now enjoys getting chapter books from the library. He still struggles with writing skills, given his fine motor problems and reduced sight.

His neurologist continually reminds us of the first day he saw him in the emergency room when he was three months old, screaming in pain and unable to be comforted or examined. He tells Jake, "You are destined for greatness" which is what Alan and I believe as well. We are so thankful not only for the health professionals that surround us with hope and help, but his teachers and the school, so dedicated to helping him succeed.

Jake (age 10) says: *I have a family that loves me and cares about me. I like having lots of brothers and sisters (mostly sisters, I always ask if we could have more brothers). I thank God for my mom and dad adopting me.*

BLESSING TIMES TWO

Less than a month after Jake's first birthday, we got a call from another social service agency in Virginia, asking if we could take two baby girls—"and if you can't take them, Mrs. Steele, we have no place else for them to go." Once again, I called Alan, who said yes. That evening, just at dinner time, two social workers arrived at our house with a 15-month-old little girl, screaming in terror, and her 3-month-old sister, who was quietly observing everything around her. The girls were brought to us with nothing but a T-shirt apiece on their bodies.

That evening, while we were signing papers for a rental property we had just purchased (our attorney,

Mike Sweeney, also our neighbor and friend, makes house calls), we had both of the girls alternately crying and feeding while we signed. Mike will never forget having to hold each one of them in turn at the kitchen table as we closed on the rental property.

We had already agreed with friends to have their ten-month-old foster daughter (whom they later adopted) with Down's Syndrome for the weekend. They were traveling out of town and were unable to take her with them. So for three days we had four babies in the home. Now I have a healthy new respect for acquaintances with quads and multiple-birth children.

Only too quickly we discovered that Tanisia (Tawnee), the older of the two girls, only stopped crying when she was held. Unfortunately, surrounded by three-month-old Taylor, twelve-month-old Jake, as well as Tawnee, this was not physically possible. After two weeks of the nonstop crying and screaming (Tawnee), compounded by Jake's torturous carrying on every time I fed Taylor (Jake had just been weaned off of his bottle and cried every time he saw Taylor drinking), not to mention three sets of diapers, I was ready to pull my hair out. The social worker called once and calmly observed, "Well, Tawnee stops crying when you pick her up, right?" This was not too helpful of an observation. A mother with three babies has only two hands, two hips, and one back.

As Tawnee finally started to settle down, and Taylor began to sleep through the night, we began to see the effects of their nomadic, homeless life before being dropped off on our doorstep. Tawnee and Taylor's mother (the girls have the same birth mother) was a "professional" woman by trade who had used drugs during both pregnancies, and was mentally challenged. She was sweet, as I came to know her during her infrequent visits with the girls, and loved them, but she was unable to care for them. The social service agency explained "All of the children, parents, and relatives for two generations have either been adopted out or been in foster care. Our agency knows this family well."

Tawnee was a serious child from the first day she came home. She was clingy, and seemed to be unhappy much of the time. She carried a sippy cup around the house with her, so we let her have an empty one between mealtimes, as her Linus blanket. The only words she could say were "cookie," "mama," and "juice." She called any female "mama", and was constantly walking around the house asking for a cookie or juice. We had her tested for delays, and she needed physical and emotional play therapy.

Tawnee was more mobile than Jake since she's four months older, but had a difficult time playing with him or with any other children around her. She couldn't be away from me, and if I was paying attention to any other child, whether it was Jake, Taylor, or another playmate, she would go into a tantrum. She and Taylor had never attached to anyone during the time they were living with their mother as they were constantly tossed from person to person, shelter to hotel to living on the street; Tawnee had also been beaten in the face just before she came to us, although her injuries were mostly healed by the time we saw her. Her face had been slightly swollen when she came to us. However, all of the back-and-forth living, never knowing where she was going to be, or who she would be with, caused her to develop Reactive Attachment Disorder. This makes her distrustful that anyone, particularly adults, will be able to meet her needs.

After much testing, therapy, and time, Tawnee has become attached to Alan and I—so much so that she is my "velcro child," always coming to look for me if I am in a different part of the house. She will probably always have food issues—she plans her day's activities around mealtimes, and the girl can eat anything, anytime, anywhere. She's our only child that doesn't have a favorite meal, because she likes everything. Alan often jokes that if someone cracks open the door to the refrigerator or pantry, she can hear it no matter where she is in the house and is in the kitchen immediately, demanding a part of whatever is being eaten or prepared. She's tall and thin, so her huge appetite does not affect her weight. She will most likely always need to feel in control of her environment.

Taylor, on the other hand, was too young to be adversely affected by all of the back and forth living. She had not been physically harmed before coming to us, although we were made to understand that she, like Tawnee, had been exposed to much domestic violence in her short three months of life. Due to the fact that she was able to attach to us right away (since she was so young and we were her only caregivers), she has not suffered any ill affects of the violence or attachment issues. For most of her life, she's enjoyed being the youngest in a large family. She is intelligent, but learned very quickly how to use her status as the youngest and as being little (she's nine, but only the size of a six-year-old, and has always been tiny for her age) to get by with as little work as possible. This started when, as toddlers, we would get the kids to clean up their toys—Taylor was always able to get someone else to do it for her. Until we moved out to the country, it was difficult to motivate her to do any type of work at all, even cleaning her room, or doing any type of homework that didn't immediately come easy to her. The private Christian school the children attend demands more of her, and she's finally learning to rise to the challenge rather than sitting on her laurels for what comes easy to her.

It's been easier to see the hand of God in His timing for Tawnee and Taylor to join our family. We needed time to grieve the loss of Hailee, yet not too much time passed before we were ready to move forward with our family. We wanted to adopt them right away. We were waiting out the requisite time, but just before their mother's parental rights were to be terminated, she was killed by a passing truck while walking across a busy street at night. As we mourned her death, we went to her funeral. Alan was a pallbearer. We met several of Tawnee and Taylor's relatives, including their maternal grandfather, who has custody of our girls' older sister, Tasia. We also met our girls' great uncle Bob, the maternal grandfather's brother (not his real name).

The social service agency had begun the paperwork and court hearings in order for us to adopt the girls. In the meantime, they called to say that their great uncle

Bob wanted custody. We were devastated; he and his wife lived in Maryland, had never seen the girls, and had never done anything to help when they were living on the street, being exposed to violence, drug behavior, and abuse. We held our breath as the social worker checked this couple.

It turned out (although we did not find out until several years after the girls' adoptions) that great uncle Bob had served nine years of his sentence for the rape of a little girl. It still gives me the creeps to know that he visits unsupervised with Tasia, my girls' birth sister, who is only one year older than Tawnee.

We knew we would be hearing more from the family members we had met at the funeral, if for no other reason than to see our girls. The morning following the funeral, the girls' maternal grandfather showed up at the social worker's desk demanding custody. This was a man that social services had twice requested to take our girls, before they came into foster care, and then after they began living with us. Both times, he refused. Virginia law requires not only that any family members who take custody of foster children be able to support themselves, but that they are either married, or single and not living with an unmarried partner. The grandfather was unemployed, and lived with his girlfriend, Tasia's caregiver, at her home. She was the breadwinner.

I have often tried to see if Tasia could come and live with us as well, but since custody had been granted (informally, not through the court system) before our girls came to live with us, there was nothing that I could do legally to overturn it. However, Tawnee and Taylor were ours, and it just took a little more time for the adoption paperwork to be finalized through court.

Alan and I are firm believers in open adoption, whatever form it takes. Tawnee and Taylor still see their birth grandmother, their birth great-grandmother, who raised their mother for a time before foster care, and their birth aunt. They have had two opportunities, in the last six years, to see their birth sister Tasia, but it's usually pretty difficult to arrange this. We make arrangements to meet with the relatives at a McDonald's near their home a couple of times per year. The girls are able to have a sense of family, of connection, that will help them as they get older. Many adopted teens go through adoption issues around abandonment. It is important for our children to know some sense of belonging.

Let me say in all honesty that it is sometimes difficult to keep up contact. Our children's birth families are pretty dysfunctional. They make plans, either with me or on the phone with our children, and do not follow through. Alan and I are left to pick up the pieces when they don't show up or a promised present does not arrive.

I don't feel any jealousy toward these birth families. I am secure, for at the end of the day, my children go home with me. They know, and will always know, that I am their mother. I respect the birth families for what they have had to give up. But, the hard part is seeing the children that remain in these families and knowing that they are in a precarious, sometimes dangerous situation. It is also difficult to listen to promises made to my kids, both over the phone and in person, knowing that what has been promised will never materialize and then trying to explain this to the younger kids, in a nonjudgmental way.

It used to be policy in almost every state that any subsequent children born to birth parents who had their parental rights involuntarily terminated, would be taken at birth. Those policies have changed nationwide. Nowadays, even if someone has had three or more children adopted out, most social service agencies allow them to keep subsequent children. This arises from the greater push for children to stay with birth family, along with the current US budget crises. The budgets for helping children are usually the first that are cut. So children are remaining in homes that are often dangerous, dysfunctional, and neglectful. Staying with birth mothers who have used drugs during pregnancies. Stuck in homeless situations, in homes with domestic violence, often with parents who have been suspected, but not convicted, of severe child abuse. These are the natural siblings of some of my children, and it is heartbreaking to watch. This is my biggest challenge.

Tawnee (age 10) says: *I like being adopted because my parents take care of me, and I learn about Jesus. I love having my older sisters around; it's always nice to get another one! I'm glad I have a family that I love so much.*

Taylor (age 9) says: *I like being adopted because I have lots of brothers and sisters, lots of animals, and I have two parents. We have a big house and I like having an older sister from Ethiopia and sharing a room with one of my sisters. If I wasn't adopted, I might have to sleep outside.*

A TEEN BLESSING

In late May of 2005, when Tawnee had just turned two, we met a young girl who would again change our lives. Evelyn was the foster daughter of friends who babysat when we were out of town, or when I needed to be in court. She was seventeen when we met her, and we were surprised and proud to be invited to her high school graduation. Due to the foster care system, she had to go to four different high schools for her senior year, which made the task of graduating even more onerous, and that much more of a sweet victory.

Evelyn spent most of the summer at our house, swimming, hanging out with the kids, and babysitting.

We grew to care about her, and when it seemed that she wasn't going to be able to stay in foster care, we offered her our home. As we were later to discover, she desperately wanted to take our offer, but felt that we were just being nice, and didn't mean it. We lost touch with her for about three months.

In the middle of January of 2006, we had to make a quick overnight business trip to Orlando and found out through our friends where Evelyn was staying. She had been "couch hopping," going from distant relatives to friends' homes sleeping on their sofas as she looked for a job. Although she was supposed to have started college the previous September, she had no one to help her with the maze of school registration and financial aid, and had given up. We asked Evelyn to come stay at our home with the kids during our trip.

While I was talking to her before we left, I found out that she was planning to move to Hawaii to take an offer to live with a boy she had known in junior high school. I was afraid for her, and asked, "Is this a decision you feel that God wants you to make?" She looked at me right in the eye and said, "No." I told her it was scary to be doing something knowing it was not God's will. "I hope you will reconsider." I realized she felt she had no other options.

The next morning, as Alan and I waited for our flight, I told him about Evelyn's plans. He shook his head, and said he felt the same way. "It will be a poor choice for her." We were not able to sit together on the full flight out, but as soon as we arrived in Orlando, as we were walking off of the plane, Alan grabbed my hand and said, "I've been thinking about Evelyn for the entire flight, and praying that God would change her mind. I think we should ask her to live with us." Since this was exactly what I was feeling, I started to cry, and told him I would call her that evening. We were both nervous that she was intent on moving to Hawaii, which sounded adventurous and romantic to a girl who had never been west of Chicago.

That night when I called to check in on the kids, I asked Evelyn. Without a moment's hesitation, she responded, "Yes, I would like that." I was shocked and overjoyed, and asked if she wanted to think about it first, but she said no, she was quite comfortable coming to live with us. I then told her about our prayers for her throughout the flight and during the day. "We asked God to grant us favor with you so that you would accept our offer of a home and a family."

It didn't take long for Evelyn to settle in. We got her into college classes that same week. Within two months, we were sure she belonged in our family, and wanted to adopt her. As we tell people every chance we get, EVERYONE needs a family, regardless of their age. The tragedy of children aging out of foster care in this country without any family or mentors who will be there for them is overwhelming. We loved Evelyn, and wanted to make sure that did not happen to her.

God planned our lives much more than we did in preparing us (without our even knowing) for a wider family. About a week before Evelyn came to stay with us, we had decided to sell our seven-passenger van to get a vehicle that had more seats (I wanted it to seat nine, Alan was content with eight). Alan had found a Tahoe, and was in the process of making the deal when Evelyn moved in. I was a little disappointed that it only seated eight, but when I drove it the first day, realized that it seated nine with the extra third seat up front. This was our nine-seater.

Unfortunately, the social service agency that had placed Jake with us did not share our excitement at adopting Evelyn. Less than a week after she moved in, an acquaintance, who disapproved of us adopting children "out of race," called social services to tell them that we had allowed an underage girl to stay with our children while we traveled out of town, and that she was now living with us. The social worker immediately told us that we had to make a choice between Jake and Evelyn, as we did not "have their permission" to house an eighteen-year-old. I made a few phone calls to discover that since Evelyn was eighteen, we did not need to ask anyone's permission. The agency was out of line in threatening to take Jake from us if Evelyn stayed. We protested, and kept both of them in our family.

The social worker was furious that she didn't get her way. The agency made it extremely difficult for us, re-interviewing Alan and I, and insisting on additional, private interviews with Evelyn (although we were never able to determine the reason). They asked us to take more psychological tests. Since they refused to pay for them ($1,200 apiece), and we had already done psychological testing in San Diego prior to Aimee's adoption, we directed them to those tests. Luckily, our idiosyncrasies were few enough. We looked fairly normal on the tests. The head of the adoption unit told us that San Diego social services recommended us highly.

Evelyn has told us that all the time she was visiting that first summer we knew her, she was glad for the four younger Steeles. They had been adopted as babies and would be able to grow up with a mom and a dad. Little did she realize that she would get to have the same mom and dad, although not that advantage. I have told her more than once, "One of my wishes is to wish that I could have raised you, protected you, and spared you pain." Even though I know that what we experience makes us who we are, strengthens us as people, and can strengthen our faith.

Evelyn was one of four siblings taken from their birth mom when she was five years old. She and her sister Jasmine moved through numerous foster homes in Chicago before living with the maternal grandmother, when Evelyn was six. They lived with her until Evelyn was ten and Jasmine twelve, when they were sent to Portsmouth, Virginia to live with their other grandmother. Evelyn was later placed back in foster care as an older teen. I am still amazed at the resourcefulness and tenacity of my daughter—four different high schools in her senior year, and yet still graduated. We are so proud of her. She has overcome adversity to become a successful and productive adult.

Evelyn graduated two years ago from US Army boot camp at Fort Jackson, South Carolina, and was one of very few girls in her barracks who LOVED boot camp. Her letters were full of descriptions of learning to be a sharpshooter and how she was the only one at night who didn't cry to go home (I don't know whether to take that as a compliment or not). We are frankly amazed that our tiny, four-foot-10 inch daughter who weighs less than 100 pounds has enjoyed being a soldier so much.

She was stationed at Fort Lee, less than two hours from us, for her post-boot camp training. Once she finished this training, she headed to the same base where her brother Kevin is stationed. We feel blessed to have her so close to us for now, although I know that it will be difficult for me as she progresses in the Army and perhaps has to be deployed to a battle zone.

Evelyn says: *At seventeen years old I felt like I became a Steele even before the courts made it legitimate. Now that I'm 26, looking back, I wonder where I would be and what I would have become if I didn't have a family I could count on, get advice from, and help guide me on the path that I'm on today.*

I've been told that the Army is strong because of each soldier, and the soldier is strong due to their family support. If things aren't right at home, the soldiers in the Army are affected. So having a family that supports and encourages me makes me want to go above and beyond — "Got Family?""

FIGHTING FOR LOVE

Life became a little miserable after encountering the social worker's wrath when she did not get her way trying to force us to make a choice between our son and our newest daughter, Evelyn. Most social service agencies give their social workers latitude in making such decisions. One social worker's bias can ruin it for a child and turn a potential adoption into a split family. So most of us put up with anything we have to in order to keep our children in our families. We were about to get the full attitude from this social worker. Any appeal we made to the agency only made it worse, and jeopardized our adoption of Jake.

The social worker, Gill (not her real name) started arriving a couple of hours late to pick up Jake for a visit with his birth mom, or alternatively, would not show up at all. Then she would show up any time, whether we were home or not, and demand that Jake be made ready for a visit. Once Gill came over while Alan and I were out of town and demanded to see Jake's clothing to make sure we were dressing him properly. The babysitter had no idea where all of his clothing was stored; the worker went back to her agency and reported that Jake should be removed from our home. There were several boxes full of new clothes for him in the closet and in our attic.

On another occasion, Gill called me while I was in an airport in Baltimore trying to get home. She accused me of lying to her about traveling, claiming she could hear Jake in the background while I was talking to her. I had been seated near a family with small children. I moved away from them to another part of the airport to converse with her. Gill reported me, again, to the agency, saying that I had to be lying because she had begun to drive by our home to see if I was there when I said I was out of town. She could see our Tahoe in the driveway, thus "proving" I was being untruthful. Alan and I both tried to explain that I took our smaller car to the airport when out of town, leaving the larger vehicle for Alan. Unfortunately, the agency backs their own, so no amount of explanation would clear our name.

Once, Gill arrived at our home for an unannounced visit to pick Jake up just as he was getting off of the bus from his preschool in front of our house. As I went to get him off of the bus, she shoved me aside, grabbed Jake, and put him, while he was screaming, into her car. "I'm taking him for a visit with his birth mom." She then stood in my driveway, and in front of her coworker and the bus driver, and began yelling, "I'm going to make sure you will never be allowed to adopt Jake, or Tawnee and Taylor." Even though the girls were from another city's agency with a different social worker.

Gill's behavior bordered on lunacy, and I was embarrassed for her, not to mention distraught because Jake was so upset and scared. I was surprised that her coworkers were not more embarrassed and had come with her to pick Jake up. Once, when another coworker joined her, they came into the foyer of our home. When I handed her Jake's diaper bag for his birth mom visit, she opened it and began tossing all of the items onto the floor and stairs in front of her. Although I had worked with social workers for years both as an attorney and a foster/adoptive parent, I had never seen someone behave this way. It was a painful eighteen months trying to work with her during the course of the hearings waiting for Jake's adoption.

Gill's dislike of us came back to haunt us just after Jake's birth mom made the loving decision to discontinue her court appeals and allow him to be adopted. The birth mother called me: "I know you are Jake's parents and that he just needs to be yours legally; so to speed up the adoption process, I'm going to drop my second court appeal." Normally, this would allow the agency to immediately file the paperwork to finalize the adoption, which in our state takes about 2 months. Instead,

Gill announced to the agency that she felt we were inadequate as parents because we were dishonest. So she blocked our adoption of Jake.

This started the nightmare roller coaster. The agency re-interviewed Alan and I, and then Evelyn, requesting and receiving all of our records from San Diego County; requesting that we undergo psychological evaluations again (at our own expense) even though we had done so in San Diego, who had forwarded them the results. Several agency workers understood that we were being treated unfairly. Fortunately, Jane (not her real name), one of the workers, contacted us after working hours from home. "You are both going to be called into a meeting later this week at the agency, and the plan is to remove Jake from you permanently."

Legally in Virginia after a child has been in the same foster home for eighteen months, the agency has to give a two-week notice and a definitive reason as to why a child is being removed. The adoptive (or foster) parents have the right to petition the court for custody. Jane was hinting that we should immediately file in court for custody of Jake. In telling us, she put her job, and her long career at risk.

Alan and I went to the meeting in defensive mode. We were accused of all kinds of things. We offered logical, and truthful, explanations for each false accusation. Finally, the foster/adoptive care director gave her real reason for this meeting: "Well, you have to understand, we are not doing *this kind of thing* anymore." Alan looked at her with astonishment. "What kind of thing are you referring to?"

"Well, placing out of race. We don't do that anymore."

Alan and I were shocked. She was admitting the departmental prejudice that we had suspected for a long time. We sat there trying to catch our breath. Finally, I said, "You know, when Jake was in the hospital and you called us and BEGGED us to take another brain-injured baby, we looked white, Caucasian, and Jake was brown. He is now three years old, and WE ARE HIS PARENTS. He is still brown, and we still look white. If you didn't want us to take him, you should have thought of that when you needed us so badly. And for the record, you all are the only people that have a problem with skin color. It doesn't matter to us, to our family, to our other children, to Jake, or to his birth mom. And it doesn't matter to the African-American judge in this case, who is assuming you are doing your job in getting his adoption completed."

We walked out of that meeting and drove down the street to the courthouse to file for custody. We knew that pending the hearing, social services could not take Jake away. In the meantime, they sent us a nasty letter. It stated that they were gong to continue the hearing for three months, during which time they would monitor us "constantly" to determine whether or not any of the accusations made against us were factual. We waited anxiously, but no one called us or came by during the three-month period.

So with no contact at all from social services, the day before the hearing, I called the City Attorney. He represented the social service agency in court, and had been intimately acquainted with Jake's case since its inception. He was shocked that there had been no communication from social services, and said, "I'll push for them to put together the adoption placement paperwork by the time of the hearing."

The next morning when our case was called at court, neither the city attorney nor any representatives from social services were available for the hearing. The judge was furious that our adoption was not final, and that no one was in her courtroom to argue the case against us. She summoned the City Attorney, who practically danced in front of her (I felt sorry for him, since it wasn't his fault) telling her that he was doing everything he could to get his client (the agency) to put the paperwork together. She told the City Attorney, "If the Steeles do not sign their adoption placement for Jake in three days, I will expect ALL of you back in my courtroom with an explanation of why this child has not been adopted by this family yet. This is a travesty, and I expect the agency to remedy it IMMEDIATELY." We breathed a sigh of relief.

We thought this would be the end of the struggle. We were wrong. We hired an attorney friend from church, an African-American, who had butted heads with this agency before and was not afraid to do it again. Charles Staples had been our attorney when we tried to keep Hailee. He loves Jesus, and genuinely loves representing children in the court system. He was righteously angry at the agency for their prejudicial stance on the difference in our races. He knew they were being unreasonable and had dragged out the adoption process too long. We argued with Social Services for another six months before the adoption papers were signed.

Finally, in August of 2007, just before Jake turned five, we celebrated with a huge adoption party for Evelyn, Jake, Tawnee, and Taylor. Over sixty friends and family came. including our pastor, who dedicated the three youngest to the Lord and prayed over them. What a joyous celebration to a long journey, especially for Jake! Buckets of fried chicken, mounds of homemade potato salad, and loads of desserts were eaten as we celebrated far into the night. Alan's brother Marty and his family were visiting, so we had the extra blessing of having more members of the Steele clan celebrating with us. It was a wonderful time for friends and family to embrace our children into our lives once again.

AN OLDER ADDITION

We had purchased a few vacation homes in Orlando (hence the business trip to Orlando some years earlier when Evelyn decided to live with us), so it was time to take the kids to Disneyworld, a prominent vacation spot for people living on the East Coast. None of the children had ever been, although Aimee had been to Disneyland in L.A. when we lived in San Diego; she was too young at the time to be able to remember it.

So our family sets out one day from our vacation home for the all-day trek to the Magic Kingdom. As busy as we were with three kids, plus Aimee and Evelyn, we were (as we usually are in public) too busy to notice other people's reactions to our family. On this trip, however, we had the three little ones in a Disney double stroller (the strollers are huge, and Taylor was tiny), plus Evelyn and Aimee tagging along beside us. At one point as I was busy studying where we were headed next, trying to make sure we had everyone together, Alan nudged me, and said, "Are you noticing people's reactions to us?" I admitted I hadn't—who had the time to look around and see who was looking at us? He laughed and said, "Watch these next people we come up to." I slowed down and tried to pay attention. With each group that passed us, the people would look at Alan and I, take a glance at Aimee and Evelyn, look down at the stroller, and then stare at the two of us again. It was pretty comical to watch people's reactions to our family over and over again!

While we were going through all these difficulties, we were blessed to add to our family again. I met Evelyn's older sister, Jasmine, at Evelyn's high school graduation, and she had come over to visit. She enjoyed Alan and his sense of humor. Alan is constantly making wisecracks, the kind that you have to think about to catch, particularly if you aren't used to his humor. Brendan, Kevin, and Kara grew up with it, so they are pretty swift on the uptake, but it always takes Jasmine a minute to figure out what he's joking about. She and Evelyn constantly tease each other about which one of them is the "slowest." Jasmine was a freshman at Hampton University when we met her. During the summer of her sophomore year, she stayed with a distant relative in New York, working and earning money to afford her own apartment. By the time school started again in the fall, Jasmine was working for Nordstrom, and getting her own apartment. We didn't realize how badly she wanted to be in a family as well, until she came over for dinner one night and asked to speak with us alone after dinner (we thought she was going to ask us for a loan). Despite her nervousness, it thrilled us as we sat down with her in our little living room/prayer room as she asked, "Will you adopt me too?"

Many people question us for adopting an adult, even for adopting an eighteen-year-old, like Evelyn. But as we repeat many times, everyone needs a family. A twenty-year-old needs someone to come home to for weekends, or Christmas vacation, or to call and say, "I need support here." Yes, Jasmine had done extremely well on her own, with family friends to help along the way. But it is more than satisfying to say, "I belong to a family."

Alan and I have worked hard to encourage both young women to maintain contact with their birth family, particularly their birth parents. They both still reside in the Chicago area. Their birth father continued to write to both girls from prison as soon as he knew they were living with us, or in Jasmine's case, living close by and that we had adopted them. I have also spoken with their birth mother several times by phone, and assured her that we were delighted to have them in our family. We also encourage the girls to keep up contact with all of their relatives in Virginia and Chicago. Jasmine visited with her grandmother in Chicago recently on a quick trip with me. A wonderful reunion for both of them. They had not seen each other in twelve years.

It is not easy to "raise" girls who have already been raised in the foster care system and with other relatives, but without a father. We are fortunate that our girls have allowed us to pour into them, in a few short years, the important issues for independent living. A work ethic, financial independence through saving and refusing to live on credit, and the importance of continued education. They both remain close to Alan, and put him on a pedestal as their father, teasing each other and our other daughters that each of them is his number one. He loves teaching them to drive a stick shift, taking them to the car auction, or just having them tag along with him at the grocery store.

A couple of years ago I was doing an assignment for a class I was taking in African-American Literature, and needed a perspective from one of my daughters. I asked Evelyn if any of her friends ever said anything to her about her parents being "white." She said no, but she was often asked, "Why do your parents only adopt black kids?"

"What do you tell them?" I asked.

"I tell them what you always say, that you adopt whomever God brings to you." That was good enough for me! (I was surprised that my daughter was actually quoting me.)

Evelyn is soft-spoken and sometimes kind of shy around people she doesn't know well. She generally likes to remain in the background when in a group or a crowd. One day, we were all talking about how people tend to stare at our family when in the public eye. We never know whether it's because there are so many of us, or because of the diversity of our skin tones. Evelyn shocked us all when she said, "I love it when we go to a restaurant and everyone stares at us. It's like we're celebrities!" We laughed, remembering that often, when people stare, we have the kids wave to them. Another time, when Jasmine was talking to a young teen girl visiting our family to evaluate if she wanted us to adopt her, she said, "It's great to be adopted, because everyone thinks you're so interesting, especially when you're in a mixed family."

Jasmine was the first of our girls to become interested in the Army, and was the one to encourage Evelyn to join. The girls had intended to go to boot camp together, but because their jobs were different, Jasmine went in about five months ahead of Evelyn. She graduated boot camp from Fort Jackson, and we were so fortunate again that her training was close to us. She is now stationed just down the street from my sister, close to the beach, and close to us. We're aware that she won't always be this close to us. She was deployed to Afghanistan last year, and it was hard for me, as a mom, to have her over there. We are so proud of her. The Army will not only pay back all of her college loans, but will pay for her to complete her graduate degree. Her goal is to be a marriage and family counselor for Army families. Kevin and Evelyn are also planning to make a career of the Army. We've encouraged them to pursue their dreams, although I'm not too thrilled about the continued prospects of combat duty, and worry each time one of them is deployed. Like Evelyn, Jasmine is small, and it's difficult for me to imagine both of my tiny girls in dangerous territory.

Jasmine was married two years ago to our wonderful son-in-law, David, just after she finished boot camp, and our fifth grandchild (and granddaughter) Grace just graced us with her presence a few weeks ago.

Transracial Adoption - We are often asked to speak on transracial adoption, and what parents should think about when adopting a child not of their race. In responding to these questions we typically ask our older daughters, and sometimes our younger kids, what is important to them.

The number one issue they always cite is HAIR. If a parent is not able to do their child's hair, they will need to commit to spending money on having their hair properly done according to what is acceptable in that child's cultural community. This applies mostly to African-American hair, but also Caucasian or Asian hair. (Before you laugh, I have several African-American friends who struggle with doing "white girls'" hair.) The practice of adopting out of race is not limited to Caucasian parents; many African-American parents adopt white children, particularly in the southern states.

And just because you know others who do not do their children's hair properly, that does not let you off of the hook. People will always scrutinize your children more carefully, if only to "prove" that transracial adoption is detrimental to the children. Adopting transracially means that you have to be a cut above others . You cannot be thin-skinned. Get used to criticism, and looks from strangers. Although we do not usually have to deal directly with rude comments, many people question whether our children belong to us. Our children's friends say things like, "That can't be your mom, she's too white!"

For their preschool and kindergarten grades, our youngest three children, Tawnee, Jake, and Taylor, attended a Christian school down the street from us. The school had all black students and teachers, and was connected with an all-black church that we attended several times. One of my friends, a parent of my children's classmates, was having lunch with me one day and the subject of transracial adoption came up. She told me that several parents had asked her (although they would not approach me directly) why we adopted only black children. She replied, "Well, I don't see you or anyone else at this school or church adopting any kids." That stopped the overt comments, though I am sure people at the school still talked about us. They were quick to let me know that they could do my kids' hair, even if they were complete strangers. I was the only mother that was approached about my children's hair (which has always been expertly done by Jasmine and Evelyn).

I asked my older daughters what their friends said. One of them responded, "My friends ask if having white parents means that we are raised differently." My daughter laughed, "Parents are the same everywhere. You get in trouble if you do something stupid, and they love you no matter what your skin color is."

Another friend indicated that she thought it was cool because it showed that we didn't care what our children look like, we just love them because of who they are. My daughters agree. I poll our younger kids periodically to ask the same question, but they say no one ever says anything to them. My older girls think it's because littler kids don't know how to express something like that, or because they don't care, whereas their older friends "think it's cool."

I used to think it was foolish for adoptive parents to want their kids to look like them, and thought it was the ultimate ego trip. (If you can't bear children who will carry your physical traits, you should look for children to adopt who will look like you.) As little as 30 years ago, adoption agencies would match adoptive parents and their children according to physical characteristics. But now I more readily understand these adoptive parents' reasoning. They want children to look like them so that they won't be asked awkward questions about adoption. It takes effort and self-confidence to teach adopted children to respond to questions they will encounter. We are fortunate in that our children just see us as mom and dad. I believe this is even more true for older teens and young adults who can freely choose adoption.

Jasmine and Evelyn have enriched our lives in a way that is hard to describe. Even though we weren't privileged enough to raise them, they have both stolen our hearts and we deeply and fiercely love them. They have blessed us so much as we convert our parent/child relationships into relating as adult to adult—the transition we make when our little girls grow up. God has truly given us gifts in Jasmine and Evelyn. We have been renewed having them in our family and lives.

Jasmine (age 27) says: *Growing up, there was never a parent to hold me, console me, or help fight my fears. I wanted to know what was wrong with me, who should I have grown up with, or who I would become? There was never a day in my life that I didn't ask myself the question "Why wasn't I wanted?" The constant filling of my heart with doubt built up to be a secret that I never let out. Going through life feeling alone, I accepted the fact that I had no home.*

But then God brought new meaning to my life. Even though I was an adult . . . being adopted has healed a spot in my heart that I never thought was possible. Having parents who care and who have been there for me through all of my strife makes a huge difference even though I received it later in my life. We may look different and I may not have been born from both of them, but ...they will always be my mom and dad.

AFRICAN BEAUTY

In the fall of 2008, Alan and I were contacted through a couple of different adoption groups we work with in our area. Would we be interested in a short-term missions trip to Ethiopia, working with orphans there? We wanted to hear more. How had the leader of the group found our names? As it unfolded, a gentleman named Dave McIlrath, out of Dallas, Texas, owns and operates several Ethiopian Guest Homes in the capital city of Addis Ababba. He has adopted two Ethiopian children, and has been instrumental in helping numerous other families adopt through that country. His guest homes are specifically set up for adoptive families and missionaries. Dave offers a modern, inexpensive place to stay while working or connecting with adoptive children. Dave had gotten our names from a conference we attended through the Christian Alliance for Orphans, an organization sponsored by Focus on the Family and Family Life Today.

We embarked on this missions trip, meeting up in Addis with 30 other people from around the U.S. and one couple from Korea. We visited baby orphanages to hold the babies; we visited many small village schools, meeting children who walked several miles each way, all barefooted, to get to school each day. We met lots of street orphans through a soccer and sports ministry there, playing with the kids, which eventually led to Alan and I sponsoring two.

The guest home housed all of us from the States. A beautiful young lady named Hanna managed it. She was the first person we met upon our arrival. Hanna is bright, energetic, and has a terrific sense of humor. She speaks English as well as Amharic, the primary language spoken in the capitol of Ethiopia. She doubled as our translator and guide as we visited the various orphanages and ministries working with street orphans, AIDs victims, prostitutes, and trafficked individuals.

Alan and I enjoyed Hanna immensely, and she was caught up in our life's story of adoption. Her goal was to become more educated in the United States and return to Ethiopia to work with orphans and ministries there. We fell in love with her, and agreed that she could come live with us, obtain a degree in the States (she had just completed her business degree, the equivalent of a

Bachelor's, in Addis), and then return, if she wished, to Ethiopia.

We had no idea how difficult it is for someone over the age of 14 (Hanna was 22 when we met her) to emigrate to the US from a developing country, even for a short, three-month visitor's visa. We tried EVERYTHING to help her get over to the States, without success. We spoke with embassy officials, State department officials, and various people in our US Senator's offices. We filled out forms, sent bank statements, letters from us and anyone who knew or worked with her from the States, invitations for her to speak and attend conferences here—all to no avail. We then began the lengthy process of trying to get Hanna here on a student visa.

About six months after we began this process, Hanna told us about a young man from Nashville whom she had met a couple of times at the Guest Home when he came through on missions trips. Chris was very interested in dating her long distance. We began emailing him, then calling, and learned that he was much interested in our girl, as we had begun to think of her, and in helping us to get her to the States. I was still working on Hanna's student visa for her to come to Virginia to go to school. Chris was assured (as were Alan and I) that this was the best route.

We were finally able to meet Chris in May 2010 while stopping off in Nashville on our way home from San Diego. He came to the airport to meet our family, and as we were stuck there for several hours, he had dinner with us. It was a natural, easy feeling to meet up with Chris as our new potential "son-in-law," since we'd been in contact with him for quite awhile before meeting, and since Hanna was so obviously enamored with him, and he with her. He was respectful to us and full of jokes around the kids.

We then made arrangements for him to fly out from Nashville to spend several days with us. We all loved meeting him and having him there, particularly the younger kids, who treated him like their older brother and climbed all over him. He confided in Alan and I that he wanted to ask Hanna to marry him when he returned to Ethiopia for his next missions trip less than a month later.

I knew Hanna loved Chris, but she wanted to spend more leisurely time getting to know him. We didn't tell her he was going to propose. We did, however, warn him that he should NOT marry her over in Ethiopia, because it is much more difficult to get your husband or wife over here than your fiancé. I can't say that I understand the reasoning, and have asked some State Department officials why, but have never gotten a good answer. At the time Chris was visiting us, we still thought Hanna would be coming over by the end of July on a student visa. Chris' plan was to be in Addis for his short-term missions trip and then spend the rest of the month with Hanna, having her fly back home with him. That way, the two of them could see each other for at least a month.

And then we got the news from Hanna that, once again, she had been denied a student visa. We were under the misimpression that once a college approved a foreign student, and all of the documents were submitted, the embassy would automatically process them with a student visa. The visa "interview" that most people from a developing nation go through actually only lasts about 45 seconds. In Hanna's interview, she was almost immediately told that she did not have significant ties to her own country to allow her to be a student in the States. We were stunned—what young student coming from another country is going to have their own car, their own house, or a high-paying job? These were the type of "ties" the U.S. embassy was looking for. We were disappointed, but Hanna was devastated. She told us, and Chris, that she didn't even want to try again as she was tired of the same denials (and, I suspect, the entire process is humiliating).

Chris planned to ask Hanna to marry him anyway, and took with him his grandmother's ring to present to her when he proposed. Hanna, however, was still skeptical as she didn't want either of them to feel that she married Chris to be able to come to the States. Alan and I told her, "Follow your heart. We want you here very much, but you need to do what you feel is right and what God wants for you." We did counsel her that if this was planned for her, she should probably go ahead and say yes now, even though they would be far apart while planning a wedding.

Chris did go back to Ethiopia, spent a month there, and asked Hanna to marry him. She said yes. All was not rosy, however, as they were still trying to get to know each other. As her friends met Chris, Hanna felt that he was not respectful of her culture and of the traditions that accompany meeting family and friends as a fiancé. Hanna sent an email: "I'm desperate to talk to you." (It is not possible for her to call the States; she has to email or send a message through Facebook, and then we call her.) I called. She was sobbing, saying, "I don't think Chris is the guy for me." They had fought and she was again afraid that she was going to marry him for the wrong reasons. I shared, "It is never a good idea to marry someone for any reason other than because you couldn't imagine your life without them." If she didn't want to marry him, we would think of another way to get her over here. We wanted her to be happy, and she was the only one who could make that decision.

Like most engaged couples, they needed to fight, to find a way to mesh their cultural differences and figure out how to work through it. This was only the first of many misunderstandings arising from cultural differences, but Alan and I are confident that God's grace will help Hanna and Chris to get through.

Hanna finally arrived in the US after three long years of trying to get her here. Chris finished his job in Nashville and moved to Virginia so that they could marry and settle here, which they did immediately. They lived with us for a few months and then got their own place near us. They stayed here in Virginia about a year, and then headed back to Tennessee for better job opportunities, which has worked out very well, although it was difficult for Alan and I to have them live so far away.

Hanna is adjusting to a life in the States very different from what she has been used to, having never seen the ocean, a grocery store, a shopping mall, and not living with indoor plumbing or an indoor kitchen. We're thankful for the computer age, which allows her to Skype her friends back in Ethiopia, and for cell phones, which allow her to make unlimited calls to the Ethiopian friends who are living here in the States as well. It has been a long, difficult struggle, but it is definitely worth it to have Hanna home.

Hanna (age 27) says: *When I was little, I wanted a big family with lots of brothers and sisters, and I used to go to my neighbor's since they had a large family. It was always a disappointment to go back to my home with no siblings and no dad. So when I met my parents in Ethiopia, it was like my dream coming true, I have a dad and a big family! I still feel like it's a dream every morning when I wake up and hear my siblings yelling "Dad!" and realize he's MY dad too!*

BLESSING AMIDST PAIN

As the summer of 2009 was ending, I woke up one Sunday morning to find a large lump in my breast. It was so big that the skin around it was starting to pucker. I immediately showed it to Alan, who suggested that I head out to the doctor's office as soon as we got home from church.

My primary care physician was at a drop-in doctor's office (Doc in the Box, as we call it), so she did not have the facilities to do any tests. Yet she was proactive, sensing immediately that this was serious. She scheduled me for tests and gave me the name of a well known breast surgeon "just in case."

First thing the next morning I was seen at Chesapeake General Hospital for a mammogram and ultrasound. During the ultrasound, I saw the lymph nodes on the screen, and asked the technician, "They don't look right, do they?" She said no, but told me that I had to stay put; the radiologist needed to see the ultrasound before I could get dressed.

When the radiologist came in, I could tell immediately that I was in trouble. I asked him, "Do I have cancer?" He said that technically he wasn't able to tell me. I bullied him into it by saying, "I'm supposed to call this breast surgeon in Norfolk. Should I try to get an appointment this week, or just whenever they can fit me in?" He said, "You can't wait more than 24 hours."

The next few hours moved slowly, as if I were walking through a fog by myself. The radiologist sent me down the hall to the Breast Center, where a patient counselor made a phone call. Within an hour, I was in the breast surgeon's office right next door to the hospital where I had been tested. She showed me my mammogram results, and pointed out that my right breast had the cancerous tumor (which looked and felt like the size of a baseball), with nothing showing on the left breast. She did a biopsy, and made an appointment for Alan and I to come in two days later to talk about my options. She also scheduled me for a breast MRI.

As scary as all of this felt, Alan and I knew that this was something we were going to have to get through and go on with our lives. There were too many children we were responsible for, too much in the way of blessings for Alan to have to raise the kids by himself.

We both knew this was a way for us to appreciate each other more, to appreciate our kids, and our life together, God's way of telling us that we needed to appreciate being ALIVE.

This isn't my attempt to sound noble in any way, because I spent much time crying in the shower, or on my bike riding by myself. We would do whatever we had to in order for me to get healthy again, and as quickly as possible.

The surgeon talked to us together about lumpectomy versus mastectomy versus double mastectomy. I know too many women who have had either a lumpectomy (just removing the cancerous mass and then going through chemotherapy) or a single mastectomy (removing the cancerous breast) only to have breast cancer in the other breast later. I asked the surgeon, "What would you do if you were in my position? What would you recommend for your adult daughters?" She immediately said she would choose a double mastectomy, removal of both breasts. We went home with a lot to think about.

The next day, I had a breast MRI. It's a humiliating process—actually most of breast cancer is—as there are constantly people feeling and checking your breasts, and I have avoided male doctors for most of my adult life. There are tests and more tests, and more doctors, and more biopsies and more tests. Those two weeks were a whirlwind of doctors, tests, and biopsies. And that MRI, humiliating as it was, also showed cancer in my left breast. This meant that I got to have another MRI, with a biopsy that was humiliating AND painful.

Cancer in both breasts that had already gone into my lymph nodes. I needed chemo first and then a double mastectomy with reconstruction. My uncle Jim is a brilliant chemist and doctor in pharmacology who has also developed several anti-cancer drugs. I called him and gave him the prognosis and the type of drugs my oncologist wanted to use in my chemo cocktail. I asked Jim, "Is there any way I can avoid losing my hair?" The answer, of course, was no.

So I entered into the world of chemotherapy. I was homeschooling our fourth-grade daughter, Aimee. I arranged for one of my dear friends, a law professor at Regent U. Law School where I often guest lectured, to come in on my chemo days and do Aimee's lessons. My sister Jennifer arranged to come up the one day a week that I would be the sickest. She would spend the day with Aimee, doing lessons and taking her out to lunch.

Alan took me to chemo in the mornings, and my mom, dad, or one of my sisters sat with me for the duration (eight hours or a little more). Alan tried to come by and bring me lunch. I soon learned it was NOT a good idea to tell him what I wanted for lunch in the morning. By the time he got there, whatever he had brought made me want to throw up. I still have a difficult time eating what used to be some of my favorite foods, like Chinese food, gyros, and steak fries because I associate them with chemo treatments.

Chemotherapy lowers your white blood cell count, which means you are much more susceptible to any type of disease. My doctors made everyone in our family get a flu shot. The day after every chemo treatment, I went into the oncologist's office for a shot to help my bone marrow produce more white blood cells. I was usually sick the day after the shot. My bones ached like I had a fever. I had to take naps every day because the chemo made me so tired. My treatments were on Mondays; by Thursday of the same week I was still feeling sick, and it would usually last through the weekend. The more chemo treatments I received, the slower the recovery. I lost my taste buds; everything tasted gross, even water, which I usually drink constantly during the day. I couldn't seem to find anything to drink that would taste OK, and the only thing I wanted to eat was rice, mashed potatoes, and chocolate (not necessarily in that order).

And, yes, my hair fell out. I was warned that it would come out about ten days to two weeks after my first chemo treatment, and sure enough, I was completely bald by the second week. In about 24 hours I went from thick, curly red hair down past my shoulders to baldness. What I didn't understand until it happened was that my hair had died. It came out in clumps in my hands, dry and brittle as straw. It even changed color when it died, from red to a lighter straw color. It didn't hurt but my scalp itched and felt sore. I bought a couple of wigs, but they were hot and itchy. I only wore them for church and special occasions like having my picture taken, a dress-up dinner, or when we were being filmed for a news show on our family. I always felt like the wigs were not placed on my head just right. I worried that they were slipping down my face or looked funny, so I was constantly self conscious. I mostly wore a pink sequined baseball cap during the day. I did my best not to let the children see me completely bald, although they got used to it, and to whatever questions were asked at school.

It was an effort to get out of bed each morning and get the younger kids up, dressed (Alan always makes them breakfast), and driven to their school and then get Aimee's lessons going. Sometimes all I could do was get out of bed. Some days Aimee had to read to me for her schoolwork. I would pick the kids up from school, and then as soon as Alan arrived home, tried to take a nap. We were so blessed by God in that our church friends, neighbors, family, and even our children's teachers all helped out with meals. Colleen Barrett, the president of Southwest Airlines, sent us huge baskets and boxes of food, steak and potato dinners from Allen Brothers, and baskets of fresh fruits and candies from Harry and David.

This is not a book about how I survived cancer; it's about adoption. It's about how God can move in our lives even in the midst of something not much fun and still change our lives for the better. This is in spite of ourselves, of what we're going through, if we'll only be obedient to Him.

In early October, after a month of chemo, we received a call from an adoption agency in Richmond, Virginia, two hours north of where we live. They were looking for an adoptive family for a girl, Cassandre, who was a sixteen-year-old high school sophmore. Cassandre had told her adoptions caseworker and the media that she did not want to "age out" of foster care. She wanted to be adopted before she left high school.

We prayed about it, we learned more about her background, and finally agreed to meet her with her adoptions worker. Due to her foster mom's time constraints, we were not able to set up the first meeting until the Saturday after Thanksgiving. I spoke to Cassandre once or twice on the phone and I got the feeling that she was excited to meet us.

Our first visit was at a Mexican restaurant in Williamsburg. The plan was to eat lunch and then head over to Colonial Williamsburg for a casual meeting. I was feeling pretty bad, so I was content when we remained at the restaurant, having such a great time sitting there getting to know one another. This was a young woman who hit it off with us immediately. We left feeling confident that if Cassandre wanted to be in our family, we were excited to welcome her.

She texted me all the way home on her caseworker's cell phone. She was excited about our next visit. We had set up a weekend visit the following weekend.

She had a blast, and later read to me from her journal how comfortable she felt, and that she fit in so easily with everyone in the family. I was surprised that she wanted to be adopted into a large family; I had often wanted to be an only child when I was growing up, and thought she might have wanted individual attention. On the contrary, Cassandre wanted to be in a large family precisely because she did not want the entire spotlight on her.

Our new daughter was orphaned in Haiti at birth, dropped off at a hospital sometime between birth and her third day of life. A nurse at the hospital who knew a Haitian couple in the States told them about her, and they wanted to adopt her. So the nurse took her home and that's where Cassandre spent the first five years of her life.

However, when she was only four, she was sexually assaulted. The adoptive parents living in the States, who had still not gotten the funds together, demanded that she be removed from the home and placed with another family. Cassandre told me later that she didn't want to live with the second family, that they treated her terribly, and that they often had nothing to eat. The children had to fend for themselves to find food by "dumpster diving"—eating from the garbage.

When Cassandre was eight and a half, she was finally adopted and entered the United States, beginning to live with her new adoptive family in Richmond, Virginia. Everything was completely new to her, from the culture to the language. She had learned a few English phrases in school before she arrived, but now it was like a whole new world, and she had to start all over again. Her new family spoke Creole, her native language, so she learned English at school and spoke Creole at home. For her, the language was easier to learn than the culture, which seemed so strange to her.

Just after her arrival in Virginia, she was in a major car accident with her new family. Her adoptive father was hospitalized with a broken pelvis. His health had already been deteriorating, but now he was in the hospital most of the time and on dialysis. He was also diabetic, and died of pneumonia soon after the accident.

The family began to crumble. Cassandre had felt

disappointment and disapproval from her adoptive mother upon her arrival. Now with the father gone, the mother's grief was overwhelming and Cassandre could do nothing right in the mother's eyes. She had never felt welcome in that family; the older brother struggled because he was no longer an only child, and the mother was too critical and grief-stricken to pay attention to Cassandre's needs. At age thirteen, the mother voluntarily terminated her parental rights, so Cassandre was put into foster care.

Cassandre lived in four different placements, including a shelter, in the three years before we met her. She was depressed. Two of the foster homes were disastrous. *"Now looking back," Cassandre says, "I appreciate every support system I had or the lack thereof because it's situations like the ones I lived through that have turned me into who I am today. All is forgiven, but not forgotten. There is really no point in hanging on to the bad things in my past; they can only hold me back, and I'm trying to move forward with my life. I've been told that I have a bright future, and I intend to fulfill my dreams and work on giving back to God what He has given me."*

Cassandre is graduating from high school a semester early so that she can enter the Marines and have her college education paid for. She is striving to be an engineer, but we are encouraging her, suggesting that the whole world is open to her, and she doesn't have to decide her entire future yet. Adopting a high school girl is never easy (add in the hormones, the baggage from their life before you, and their struggles to discover themselves and how they fit into the world God made them for).

We've had our share of struggles with Cassandre. We see great things for her as she prepares for her future.

Cassandre (now age 20) says: *Being adopted is like starting my life over again, especially since I'm older and had a choice in my family. Not many people have the opportunity to have that new start in their teen years.*

A TWO-IN-ONE BLESSING

At the time we met Cassandre, I was also able to meet the young lady who was staying with her in her foster home, her foster sister, Keyunda (Kiki), who was 17. In the spring of 2010, after Cassandre had lived with us for about five months, she told me Kiki was experiencing problems in her foster home. Would we consider allowing her to live with us? Alan and I prayed about it, but were skeptical; we needed to find out more information about her from the Richmond social service agency who had handled Cassandre's adoption.

I began speaking with Kiki by phone, and also placed calls to her social worker. Kiki had run away from her foster home by this time, and was living with various friends in the area, but was not being forthcoming as to where she was. She did not want to stay in foster care. Her social worker was not able to give me too much information since I was not officially related to her in any way, but agreed to consider us as an alternative foster placement once Kiki contacted her.

I encouraged Kiki to contact her worker to reveal where she was living. She was unwilling as she was at the end of her senior year of high school. She wanted to go to the local prom and participate in her after-graduation parties. The social worker thought that Kiki's intentions were to keep herself hidden until her eighteenth birthday in July.

We continued to pray, but only heard from Keyunda sporadically after the spring. I told the social worker, "We'll revisit the idea of her living with us if she materializes again, but if she turns eighteen during that time, she will still have to abide by our house rules." Alan and I have always maintained that once our children turn eighteen and are out of high school, they must follow our home rules if we are to continue providing for them. A few of our children have decided, with our help, that living on their own was preferable to living under our rules. Some have then returned, deciding that our rules might have been worth it after all. The rules are fairly simple: Keep your room and the bathroom you use clean; do your own laundry and pick up after yourself; let us know if you'll be home for dinner; help around the house (meals, dishes, younger siblings); remember you're in a Christian home (no drinking, smoking, drugs, or sex).

And then suddenly, at the end of August, as I was sitting next to the sea for my last beach-day-by-my-self until the following summer, I received a call from Keyunda. Could she come and live with us right away? She had turned eighteen, and true to her social worker's predictions, had signed herself out of foster care. This was after she had finally been "caught" during her run-away months, and sent to a shelter. We hoped she would be sent to our home immediately, but her social worker had decided she needed psychological testing first. To this day I am not sure how much of that testing was ever done.

The following day was a Saturday, and I was taking the other girls to Richmond for the day. Kiki was plan-ning to spend the night with her maternal aunt, who would allow her only one night. She was now complete-ly homeless, and asking if we would take her in and oh, by the way, she was pregnant. I called her social worker and was told that she would get back to me the follow-ing week with more information on Kiki's background. Alan and I agreed that we would take her in on a trial basis, provided that she could comply with our house rules, and with whatever her social worker would re-quire of her. This would allow her to get started in col-lege and give her the ability to be able to move out on her own.

I picked Kiki up at her aunt's home the next morn-ing. As we were loading her few items of clothing into the car, her aunt cautioned her that this was "the end of the line, your last opportunity. These people are willing to take you in and help you; don't mess it up". When I asked her aunt privately why Keyunda couldn't stay with her, she said something to the effect that they didn't get along, which Kiki later confirmed.

Keyunda had been raised since she was three weeks old by her grandmother. Her birth mom was caught up in drugs, and Kiki had drug withdrawals as a baby, having been born addicted. Her birth father was unknown. When her grandmother died, at the age of fourteen she was put into foster care, initially with some close family friends of her grandmother's. They soon felt that they were too old to care for her, and she was sent to a shelter until a foster home could be located. She was placed in a series of foster homes, none offering a permanent place.

Keyunda met her birth mother for the first time when she was sixteen, and says it was not nearly as dramatic as she thought it would be. "Here was someone I didn't know, and it didn't seem to matter that I was related to her." Kiki was was left with the impression that she would hear from her birth mom again. She never did. "I'd still like to develop a relationship with her." I think she feels more confident to do so now that she has a family.

Keyunda freely admits that she was not cooperative in any of her foster homes. Apart from normal teen girl issues, she felt "what's the point in trying to comply and develop a relationship, because sooner or later you have to move again." She gave her last foster mom such a hard time, then ran away, tired of never having her own family.

I was sad that Kiki had not taken us up on our offer earlier. We immediately got her started on prenatal care as well as enrolling her into college and helping her to get a job. She started out working at a local deli and smoothie shop, Tropical Smoothie, and then began work at the local YMCA doing child care. She was pretty cooperative, knowing that she needed to comply with our house rules. And she needed to grow up pretty quickly, as she was to be a new mom soon.

Keyunda made a smooth transition into our family, helping with the the younger kids and learning how to live in a house with annoying siblings. She gets frustrated sometimes, knowing that she's had to grow up more quickly than she wanted to, because she had first one, then a second child (two more granddaughters for us!) who count on her. It's great that she's content to have a family with a mom and dad. Recently in an interview with CBN News, she described having parents. "It's like a Christmas present that I prayed for but never thought I would get." She is the Christmas present to us, as are both of our granddaughters: Jordyan, now two and a half, and Jayde, now seven months.

Keyunda (now age 21) says: *I enjoy being in a large family because it's like a reality TV show 24/7! Being adopted even at eighteen is great because I finally have stability. I like having a dad for the first time in my life because I have someone I can look up to who can show me what God's love is like, and a mom who will talk to me even if she's busy.*

A NEW EXPERIENCE AND CHAPTER FOR US

At the beginning of the summer of 2010, as we were praying about Keyunda and waiting to hear whether she'd be part of us, we received a call from the Social Service agency in Roanoke, Virginia regarding one of their little girls. A valley city nestled between the Blue Ridge and the Allegheny mountain ranges, Roanoke is about a five-hour drive from where we live. Their agency had been experiencing a shortage of foster families for some time, and so had placed their foster children with foster and adoptive families all over the state.

This little nine-year-old girl was named Callee. She

had lived in the same foster home since she was three, but the family was unwilling to adopt her or even keep her in their home; they had wanted her removed for over a year. They were not, in the two adoption workers' minds, the best family for her.

Callee has mental challenges (the new politically correct term is intellectually disabled) as well as autism. She had lived with this foster family in a small town about an hour outside of Roanoke for these six years, and had never received any kind of therapy. The social worker had received several inquiries about Callee from families considering adoption. They were all scared off when told the extent of her mental incapacities. Would a family be willing to have her live with them the rest of her life? It is a huge commitment, and not one to be taken lightly when considering adoption. Fortunately, we were required to sign paperwork for both Aimee's and Jake's adoptions to indicate that we knew there was a potential that either of them would not be self-sufficient (which is not a concern at all for us, given the way God has miraculously blessed them both in their development). We were familiar with the possibility of a long-term commitment, which wasn't off-putting to us.

We prayed about it and continued to talk to the workers over the summer. Because of the distance and Callee's limited mental capacity, we would try to do a visit with her before she came to live with us, possibly at the end of the summer, before school started. However, the workers told us they would have to do it in the middle of September, transferring her to our home by the end of September.

Things change rapidly in our lives when God moves. The same day that Kiki called to ask if she could come to live with us, Callee's social worker called to say that they had to remove her from the foster home. Could they bring her to our home the following Monday?

I called Alan to let him know, and we spent the weekend welcoming Kiki into our family and preparing for Callee at the same time. We felt blessed that we had another week before school started, so she could start fresh with all of the other new kids after Labor Day.

Unfortunately, her foster parents had not prepared Callee at all. Her adoption worker picked her up early that morning. When she got in the car, Callee asked, "So, where are we going today?" The worker was stunned that the job was left to her.

We were excited to greet her, ready to face challenges of a different nature. Callee is only about one and a half to two years behind her peers academically; however, she has what is termed a receptive-expressive language delay. Her disability is along the lines of severe autism. Basically, she is unable to process who, what, when, where, how, and why questions, and has been tested as being on a two-year-old level for this part of her communication skills. So it is difficult for her to interact with peers, siblings, or parents. She will ask the same question numerous times in a row. She will answer a question with something completely off of the subject, such as, "Callee, how was school today?" "Mom, do you like frogs? Was Thomas Jefferson's hair long or short? Can we invite him over for Thanksgiving dinner?" She is unable to communicate in the most basic way with others, so often, when a sibling compliments her on her appearance, her standard response is, "Leave me alone!"

Our sweet daughter had a rough start in life. She was originally brought into foster care at the age of three with severe lead poisoning, after being homeless for most of her short life. Her birth mother used crack, marijuana, and alcohol during her pregnancy, was HIV positive, and at the time Callee was put into foster care, she was incarcerated. The named birth dad (whom Callee was originally named after) had taken a paternity test, which turned out negative, so her birth father is completely unknown. When she was about seven years old, Callee was able to visit with her birth mother in prison, but didn't know who she was. There were several relatives who originally were interested in taking custody, but they either became incarcerated or were turned off by her special needs.

The foster dad and the older foster brothers barely tolerated Callee. She has therefore had a difficult time transitioning to a loving father. Alan has worked hard, and continues to work, on his relationship with Callee. We have seen a little progress, particularly if Alan makes a point of asking her to go to the store with him, or to sit next to him at dinner or while watching television. She has play therapy once a week, as well as an in-home therapist, so she is learning how to relate a little more to others.

Through therapy, we have discovered that Callee has most likely been sexually abused. It is heartbreaking to us, and frustrating to realize that someone has taken advantage of her. The perpetrator knew she was unable to express herself to tell what was going on. We are vigilant, and will always have to remain so, to protect her from those who would take advantage of her, given her limited intellectual ability. As her teacher at school has reminded me, "Callee is a cute child, and she's going to be a gorgeous teen and young adult."

She is a blessing from God, all on her own. In spite of her disability, she is content to play outside every day. She will spend hours with the animals, just standing near them and talking to them. We have alpacas, mini horses, a mini donkey, and a mini pot bellied pig, as well as a therapeutic riding program on our small ranch, and it's been a blessing for Callee. She is never bored, because she can always entertain herself. She'll ride bikes by herself, sit by the pool and swing, or play basketball. She can play on a limited basis with our other children, and they are learning, with grace, how to handle her inability to communicate. It's not always easy to get the younger kids to be kind, because they think since she's bigger and older, she should be their "big sister." They are quickly realizing that in reality, they are "older" than she, and try to help her overcome her disabilities.

Aimee, who is now fourteen, has stepped up as the older sister and Callee's roommate. She is happy that they share clothes, although she complains on the nights that Callee sings every song she knows and keeps her awake. Justin Beiber is Callee's current favorite, although she is still convinced she's going to marry Michael Jackson. The other kids are usually quick to point out that he's deceased. We are so fortunate God has given us children who have a heart for helping the underdog. Even the older girls, who would normally be annoyed by Callee's constant questions, take the time to help her with simple tasks and to kid around with her about her aggressive retorts to simple questions. (Question: "How are you, Callee?" Callee: "Leave me alone! Stop bothering me!") We are thankful that the older girls are willing to work with us, and with the counselors, to find out how we all, as a family, can best help Callee to be a content child growing in the knowledge and grace of the Lord, as much as she is able to.

Alan and I have learned so much from Callee and the other mentally challenged kids in her class, as well as her Special Olympics teammates. Callee has developed special friendships with two girls from church with Down's Syndrome, and they often come over to swim or be around the horses (Callee will ride, but her friends are still a bit nervous around the bigger animals). Callee's favorite horse is Favre (named after the football player Brett Favre), whom she has dubbed as her own. She has also taken charge of one of our alpacas, a beautiful white male named Rembrandt. We have enjoyed getting to know mentally handicapped children in a way we never expected.

Callee and her friends are simply grateful to be in each others' company, and they are a lot of fun to be with. There is so much less drama and competition. Alan and I love listening to them converse when they are not aware we're within earshot; it's always fascinating to hear how they try to connect with each other in their own ways.

Callee's two friends are from a family of thirteen children, eight of whom have Down's Syndrome and are adopted. We have attended the same church and adoption fellowship groups for years, but have gotten to know them better through Callee's friendships with the girls, who are ages fourteen and eighteen. They attend Sunday school with Callee and the other younger children.

This family feels a strong calling from God to reach out to the special needs children of the Ukraine, so they have an adoption and orphan ministry to that country. Several of their children have been adopted through Ukraine, and now that some of the more stringent laws on age have been relaxed, they are looking to adopt yet another ten-year-old Ukrainian daughter with Down's Syndrome. God has a special place for these children in our friends' home, in their hearts, and in their ministry.

WHEN IT RAINS, IT POURS

As you may have guessed, during summertime social workers really work to get their adoptable children placed in a permanent home. During the summer of 2010 we had numerous calls for more children to consider adopting. One was for a set of fifteen-year-old twin girls from South Carolina; another for an eight-year-old girl in Virginia Beach, close to where we live, who had been severely traumatized. Yet another for sibling teen girls in Los Angeles. We considered these children; we prayed about them and even met with the social workers. In each case, we decided that our family was not the ideal one for these children.

Then in mid-summer another Virginia social work-er contacted us. Ciara from Fairfax County (Northern Virginia, where I grew up) was currently living in Norfolk in a residential treatment center for teens. I called Ciara's social worker. As the worker and I spoke, Ciara was just about to be moved from Norfolk to Hampton, Virginia, about a thirty-five-minute drive from our home, and where our daughter Jasmine has been living. She was being moved to a more restrictive residential facility; the hope was that she would do better there in receiving treatment and in accepting adoption.

Ciara had a difficult time disconnecting from her birth family, even though she had been in foster care since she was young. She was afraid if she was adopted that she would no longer be a part of her sisters' lives, one three years younger and one five years older. Her younger sister had been adopted several years before into a family that was initially to take both girls. They were unable to keep Ciara as her behavior was too dis-ruptive. She was not ready to be with a new family. Her older sister had been pressuring her to wait until she was eighteen and then move in with her and her three children, hoping she would stay institutionalized and not be adopted. This just added more stress to Ciara to have to choose between her birth family and adoption.

I met Ciara with her social workers in October of 2010. It took that long for her to be stabilized in her new residence, get a good start with counseling, and get to the point in her life where she would be ready to receive a family's love and unconditional acceptance. Ciara was in an inpatient youth facility, a behavioral treatment hospital for kids and teens. We met in a large, open conference room, not the most comfortable place for a start, but the only private area available. At the time we met, she was excited about the idea of having a new family, yet still apprehensive. Would she "mess up again" and lose her last chance at a regular life? Alan and I began meeting with her at visiting times on weekends, often bringing one of the other children with us so that Ciara could slowly get to know all of us in a neutral setting. We would get together with her during the center's visiting hours on Sunday afternoons, driving the 45 minutes from our home every weekend. We usually met in their cafeteria, where other families were meeting with their children as well. While it wasn't private, it was the only place we could try to get to know one another, all the while playing card games, coloring, or doing puzzles. We also started meeting weekly in family counseling sessions with Ciara and her counselor.

We were excited when she was given permission to spend Thanksgiving Day with us. Her counselor thought it best if she came to our home for dinner on the Wednesday before Thanksgiving to make the actual holiday less stressful.

Ciara took to everyone immediately, leaving almost as soon as she arrived with the older girls to go to the "hair store," a popular shopping expedition in our home, since all of the girls needed their hair done regularly. She spent time with the older girls up in their room while they did hair before dinner, getting to know them and having a blast. Wednesday night was taco night, a hands-on-meal (in other words, every man and woman for himself or herself). She later described it as a great way to see how we all fended for ourselves during a meal (you would have to experience it to understand the ordered chaos).

And then of course, there was Thanksgiving Day. I was busy getting the traditional dishes prepared, so Alan picked Ciara up and once she arrived home, she joined in with the older girls immediately as I delegated chopping, slicing, and making dips. The younger kids ran in and out, helping with setting the table and trying to taste everything, doing the occasional "stir" so they could say they made something for the dinner.

Normally, since we've lived in Virginia, Thanksgiving is spent here at our home with my parents and at least one of my sisters and their families, sometimes both. I am the oldest of three girls; Alan is the second of four boys. My sisters each have two kids, Denise has two girls who are Cassandre's age; Jennifer has two boys who are Aimee's age. However, this year, my father had just completed knee surgery and was unable to leave home. Our brood is too large and too rambunctious for my parents to have to their home for Thanksgiving, so we just had all of us, including my cousin from Wales and her husband. This was perfect for Ciara, who needed to start slowly with meeting and fitting into our family.

Our primary Thanksgiving tradition is to go around the room and hear each person offer at least one thing that they are thankful to God for. "I'm thankful for hair," I said. Everyone knew that I meant I was thankful that God had healed me of cancer, and allowed my life to continue. I was close to tears as it became Ciara's turn. I was nervous to put her on the spot, but she jumped in with ease: "I am most thankful to God for a second chance at a family who will be there for me and accept me for who I am, no matter what." No one could have scripted it better. I found out later that Ciara had never even been to a Thanksgiving dinner where everyone sat down together and ate.

The following weekend, the staff at the hospital where Ciara was staying waited until Saturday morning to tell her that she could spend all day with us. Their thought was that if they let her know ahead of time, Ciara would somehow sabotage the day pass through bad behavior, as she was still pretty fragile emotionally. She still believed that she was unworthy of a family loving her, and that she was destined to "screw it up" so that we would eventually give up on her. Because she had so little self-worth, she had a tendency to act out when she felt the pressure of coming into a new family and a new life. We had a relaxing time all day Saturday. Since I had just had my last surgery to reconstruct my breast two days earlier, I was trying to take it easy. That being said, with a large family, a Christmas parade, and a new child in the home, I overdid it as I usually do, and was pretty wiped out by the end of the night. There was snow during the parade, which made it a little more magical for everyone, but it was hard to take Ciara back to the residential treatment center later that night. It would be several more days before we could see her.

We continued to visit all through the Christmas holidays, including Christmas day. Ciara said, "This is the best Christmas I have ever had." We had just "adopted" a horse, making it our third. "This is Ciara's horse" we announced to give her a special Christmas and make sure she knew she was wanted and special. Ciara, Kiki, and Callee also received special silver and crystal name bracelets, which we get for all of our daughters.

Each of our children receives three Christmas gifts from Alan and I, since that is how many the Magi brought for our Savior after His birth. And then, of course, they have their stockings, from "Santa." We have never told our children that there is or is not a Santa—whenever one of them asks if Santa is real, we repeat, "Santa is the expression of Jesus' love for us at Christmastime." I'm sure they have learned over the years that it's our way of not answering the question directly, but we want them to understand that the ONLY meaning of celebration at Christmastime is the Savior's birth.

Of Ciara's three gifts, the mare she received was the biggest surprise. We blindfolded her and drove her over to the stables around the corner from our home where we board our horses. She was absolutely thrilled. I let her know that since Nutmeg was her horse, and because she was blind, Ciara was to be extra careful in taking care of her. We hope that this will be therapy for her, caring for and learning to ride a horse with a disability. Nutmeg is a wonderful lesson horse, despite her blindness, and has been part of the miracle of Ciara's healing.

Ciara was severely neglected as a child. Her birth parents were both involved with drugs, and her birth mother spent most of Ciara's growing up years in prison. Ciara and her sisters had lived with their grandfather and their aunt in a home that resembled a hoarder's paradise. One of her struggles continues to be that she is unused to living in an environment where cleanliness is expected. As she has readily explained, "No one has ever taught me how to clean before." Ciara was basically responsible for the care of her younger sister, and there were numerous gaps in their school attendance. Additionally, Ciara was exposed to domestic violence, much of it perpetrated on her. She remembers her birth father only coming home to her grandfather's house infrequently, but it was always accompanied by beatings for her and her sisters.

Ciara was originally brought into foster care just before her tenth birthday. Her first foster placement was with her sister, but it didn't last long. Ciara was so used to parenting her sister, she was unable to let the foster parents do their job. She was then put into a group home. About a year later, she was again given a new foster home with her sister, with a family that wanted to adopt both girls. However, Ciara's resentments at the family not being her birth family made it impossible for her to fit snugly into their lives. They adopted her sister, and she once again found herself in an institution for another year. She had another short stint with a foster family that only lasted a couple of months, and then it was back to an institution for another two years. She grew up, for five years, in an institution.

Such is the tragedy of children who aren't able to stay in a foster home due to their behavior. They either end up going from home to home to home, never finding a true family, or end up in institutions. We have explained this to Ciara and assured her she now has a chance to grow up in the few years she has left as a child, cherished by God and her family.

She has confided, "I'm most excited about having a loving dad who is active in my daily life." As with many foster situations, Ciara's limited foster placements were with female heads of households or with absentee fathers. She is learning how to relate to a father who loves all of his children and enjoys bantering with her about everyday things in her life. Although Alan's sense of humor is a little off the wall, Ciara gets him completely, and enjoys joking right back with him.

Many people believe that if a neglected and abused child is loved enough, they will overcome challenges. However, even more than love, a child with baggage needs consistency, and the knowledge that no matter what, his or her family will not give up on them. God has challenged us with being consistent in our commitment to Ciara. She can be verbally abusive, physically violent, and has, on three occasions, given false reports about us to the authorities. This has caused her removal from our home to a nearby group home. We have not given up on her being in our family; however, we are realistic enough to know that she may never be able to truly bond and live within a family. She has now just turned nineteen, and we continue to hope and pray that she will be able to commit herself to us as much as we are committed to her, even if we cannot have her living in our home. We know she needs a family she can call her own and who will be there for her no matter what she does or how she reacts, rather than responds, to family life.

Ciara communicates best by writing, and this is what she says: *"This is my first Christmas that I get with an outstanding, wonderful family. You all are the best thing that has ever happened to me. I am so happy that I get this absolutely great chance to live with a family that is so committed in taking me as their own. I love all of you so much."*

SONG OF REBEKAH

As I've previously mentioned, the late spring and early summertime is the prime season when we get calls or contacts from different agencies regarding children. We began speaking with an agency in the Southwestern part of Virginia in the spring of 2011 regarding a special teen girl, now known as Rebekah. She had been in numerous placements since coming into foster care when she was around eight years old, including several mental health hospital and residential care centers. This meant that she had some significant traumas she had been dealing with, causing much emotional pain. She also had an intellectual functioning challenge, a lower-than-average IQ.

We chatted through email and phone with Rebekah's adoptions worker throughout the rest of 2011 while she was moved to a group home just two hours from where we lived. Alan and I continued to pray about adding her to our family, and in January of 2012, the two of us made the trip up to the group home to meet her for the first time. She was very anxious to be adopted, anxious to be living with a family, and had been bugging her adoptions worker for over a year to find her a family. She was very excited to meet us. We spent about half of the day getting to know her, meeting with the worker and with the staff at the group home, and agreed to meet again with her and have her meet our family.

The children had a day off of school later that month, so we drove up to meet with Rebekah and have lunch. The following weekend she came to visit, which then became a regular weekend trip for her for the rest of the spring until school ended. We also participated in several family counseling sessions with her at the group home. By the time school ended for summer break, Rebekah came home to be a part of our family.

Rebekah has a close relationship with her maternal grandparents, who, unfortunately, were unable to care for her once she was taken from her parents' home as a young child. She had been repeatedly exposed to domestic violence, watching her father beat up her mother regularly. She still remembers the times her mother had to be hospitalized, and can describe in vivid detail cowering under a table, closing her eyes, and praying to God that her father would stop. Later, as the fighting got more intense, Rebekah's mother would decide to leave, or attempt to make her father leave. The catalyst for Rebekah being taken from the parents was when her father came to her elementary school with a loaded gun, threatening everyone at the school in his attempt to take Rebekah and kidnap her. Her grandparents have described the lack of care for her over the years, as well as the parents' attempts to placate her by giving her anything she wanted, particularly in the area of food. This resulted in an overweight child, which has continued into her teen years. Rebekah is a tall, beautiful teen girl with doe-like brown eyes and amazingly lustrous, thick hair, weighing just under 300 pounds.

Many studies have been done on trauma and its effects on brain development and brain delays. Some of these studies have also proved conclusively that when children are exposed to domestic violence, it is as if the violence was perpetrated on them; the effect on them emotionally and on their brain development is the same. Rebekah's struggle with the trauma in her life, coupled with her lower IQ, has caused her emotional and intellectual age to be that of an eight-year-old. This makes it difficult for her to be able to appropriately express emotions, as well as to be able to adequately function on a high teen level, both at school and generally in her life. She also has many of the symptoms that Tawnee and Callee struggle with through Reactive Attachment Disorder, although we believe that hers is more likely caused by limited intellectual functioning and the inability to relate to having a loving family outside of her biological parents. While it takes some children many years (into adulthood, oftentimes) to be able to sepa-rate their parent's love for them from the fact that their parents' are unable to care for them, if a child is "stuck" at a younger age emotionally, they continue to fantasize about their birth parents. Rebekah has that struggle. She will often talk about what changes she will make in her life as soon as she turns eighteen, such as moving "back home" with her biological parents, even though she will chronologically only be in the beginning of her senior year of high school. Her grandparents have as-sured her that her birth parents have a daily struggle to survive themselves, and that they probably couldn't even take care of her for a weekend, much less have her live with them. Her birth mom continues to be hospi-talized by the abuse perpetrated by her birth dad, and continues to threaten to leave him, although that hasn't happened yet.

With the exception of Jake and Callee, who both need the services of the special education classes through the public school system, our children enjoy the amazing wraparound love and caring from a spe-cial private school that is in our local area. They have loved our kids, taken them in, and nurtured them in the way only a small private Christian school can, giv-ing them extra academic help and support as much as possible. Rebekah receives as much or more academic support in this environment as she would in a special education program in the public school, with the added advantage that the teachers and staff surround her with love and caring. To leave this wonderful school envi-ronment would be detrimental to her educationally and emotionally; further, she doesn't have the intellectual capacity to make this decision as a part of her future. Nevertheless, she continues to assume, even when we attempt to bring her to reality, that at eighteen, her life will change, she will "go back" to her family of origin, and that she will be able to live with them and be provided for.

In the meantime, we are getting supports in place for her to have a full-time job and assistants who will help her to live on her own, as her "diploma" through this high school will be a certificate of attendance. Most children with intellectual disabilities have this struggle; while they are allowed to stay in school until they are twenty-one, if it is not feasible for them to be able to complete a high school diploma, the added time isn't productive for them when they can be working at a factory job or something that will bring them some income and a sense of contribution and independence. Rebekah longs for a job, so we are beginning the process now, hoping we can secure something for her while she is still in school that will continue in her adult years.

She also wants to do the things that regular teens accomplish: driving, getting a regular job (she's not as picky as many teens, in that she would be happy to work at McDonald's or babysit for money), wanting to be a cheerleader, doing teen things with friends. The real world for her is very different from what so many teens can accomplish and experience because of her emotional and intellectual disabilities. Although we acquired a private course for her to take to learn to drive, she wasn't able to pass the basic written work needed to move on to get her learner's permit. When she talks about wanting to be a cheerleader or be hired as a lifeguard, she's not able to comprehend that you actually have to be able to do the jumps and gymnastics required for cheering, or that you have to be able to swim across the pool to be a lifeguard. To be able to work at McDonald's, you have to be able to know the denominations of bills and change (in our computer age, you don't actually have to be able to make change on your own, just read what the computer register says). She talks about which college she wants to attend, though she won't be able to get a full high school diploma. And although she wants to be able to earn money babysitting, she's only emotionally at an eight- or nine-year-old level, so leaving her with younger children is not an option. These are the realities we struggle with, along with her, through her everyday life of attempting to be a teen chronologically while being a child intellectually and emotionally.

One struggle that many adoptive parents of teens face is how to help their children with the healing process of the wounds suffered from years of trauma, when there are so few years left with them at home. We really only have our children for a short time—some of us only for two or three years! While we can encourage them through therapy, often the process is a much longer one than parental influence can provide for; as the children turn 18 and 19, they are looking to become independent, often hoping to leave home as soon as possible. Once they are out of the house, all we can do as parents in the arena of therapy and help for our children is to encourage them to continue the process. So the detrimental side of teen adoptions is really twofold: the amount of trauma and possible abuses they have experienced is heightened since we have had less time with them and they have had more time to experience trauma, for instance, than babies have; and the fact that they are home for a smaller amount of time for us to work with them on the healing process is a negative effect for both the child and the family trying to help her.

Rebekah has a sweet disposition and is always ready to volunteer in any way she can, both at home and in the community. Her disability doesn't stop her from trying new things, being friendly and helpful to others, and engaging them in a limited way in social discourse. We know that God is teaching us an infinite amount as we continue to be blessed by parenting her!

Rebekah says: *I've always wanted a mom and dad who would take care of me and support me. I love the animals we have at home. It's weird having a big family with 15 kids, but I love it, and I feel safe here at home.*

WITH LIBERTY AND JUSTICE

At the time we first heard about our daughter Cal-lee, we knew her birth mom had just given birth to another girl. I was surprised at first that Roanoake Social Services, which was in charge of us adopting Callee, did not immediately take Justice into foster care, as had been the norm when another child was born to someone whose kids have been removed and adopted. We soon realized that with the budget cuts and financial crises not only statewide but nationwide, the societal pendulum has swung back toward leaving children with their families of origin and hoping for the best. Additionally, Callee's birth mom made it more difficult because she left Roanoke, where she had been incarcerated and from where Callee had been taken, and moved to Norfolk to have the baby. We told Roanoke that if Justice were ever to be taken into foster care, we would like to be contacted and given the opportunity to have her with us, as we felt it important for the girls as siblings to be able to be raised together.

Almost a year later, I was speaking at a conference in Roanoke and attempted to track down Callee's birth mom (we'll call her Sandy) through the Social Service agency. She had returned to Roanoke (which I knew), but we'd had no contact with her before. Miraculously, as God's plans always are, I was able to do some sleuthing and get a message to her at one of her former homeless shelters, and she contacted me after my search for her of about 24 hours.

When we first started speaking, Sandy almost immediately began crying. I felt awful, assuming no one had told her that Callee was adopted. She assured me that she knew, and that she was crying because she was so happy that Callee was with a family who loved her. I knew she hadn't seen Callee for about four years, and that the last visit had taken place in prison when Callee was about six and was brought there by her foster mom.

We immediately arranged to see each other. I had brought our daughters Cassandre and Ciara to the conference with me, but they had their own activities they were doing that afternoon, so I set off to find Sandy (this was in the day before GPS technology, so all I had to rely on was her sense of direction, which turned out to be excellent!). It seemed that the hotel we were staying in was only about five minutes from a home where she had been sleeping on the floor for about a week, having just left another homeless shelter.

Callee's little sister was named Justice, and she was as adorable as her name. The first time I laid eyes on her, I felt like I was seeing Callee as a baby. This was especially exciting to me since we had not been able to obtain any baby pictures of Callee—there were no pictures or mementos given to us from Callee's previous life, although we had asked for them repeatedly from the agency and from Callee's former foster parents.

Justice had just begun to walk and was toddling over to me as soon as I pulled up to the house. There was a small front yard, and it was a tiny house, from which people were constantly coming in and out as we sat together on the grass and talked.

If Sandy has ever held down a job, it hasn't been in the last twelve years. She was in prison from the time Callee was three until about a year or so before I met her, giving her time to get released and almost immediately become pregnant. Although I didn't learn as much about Callee's previous history as I would have liked that day, I pieced it together little by little in the months ahead. For the time being, it was a gorgeous day, and we sat on the grass and played ball with her beautiful toddler girl and enjoyed the sunshine and meeting each other.

I had pictures of Callee on my phone, which I was happy to share. Sandy cried all over again just seeing the pictures, and described the last visit they had together at the prison. She was currently living from floor to homeless shelter to park bench to hotel (when a local agency would cover one for her to help with her homelessness), and did not seem interested in finding employment. She told me she hoped to move to another city or perhaps another state to better her circumstances, but she did not seem to have any clear picture of how to make things different for herself, other than to find someone different who would take her in and help her make ends meet using the resources social services could provide to her. Now that I've known Sandy for a couple of years, I have come to realize that she is someone who drifts, and will probably never hold down a job. I know she has never worked since Callee was born, and she has as many excuses for not finding a job as there are days of the week. Luckily for her, she has learned how to work the social service system so that she can survive, albeit just barely.

Justice's prior life was not only nomadic, which has done nothing to engender permanency or stability for a young child, but was full of domestic violence. Sandy has been in volatile and endangering relationships since Justice's birth. As a newborn, Justice was involved in the first of many domestic squabbles, which continued until a few weeks before her third birthday. This first major domestic quarrel involved Sandy being pushed into a wall while holding Justice; the birth dad was charged and sent to jail, while Sandy was treated at the hospital. Subsequently, birth dad was jailed at least four other times that I am aware of, with a hospital visit in each instance for Sandy—all witnessed by Justice.

Unfortunately, the violence hasn't been limited to

Justice's birth dad, but has continued with other men that Sandy has hooked up with, mostly in the hopes of a place to stay. Sandy's rap sheet includes a little bit of everything—forgery, robbery, prostitution, drug charges, numerous petty theft incidents. Although she was quick, when we met, to exclaim that she would never do anything to land herself in a situation involving incarceration again, she has since called me on several occasions to ask if Justice can live with us for a brief period of time while she is locked up. I spent a lot of time trying to convince her that Justice was better off living with us rather than just staying here for a few weeks at a stretch, then going back to the nomadic life of homelessness each time Sandy was set free, but it wasn't until just before Justice turned three that her world changed forever.

Sandy was in yet another violent argument with Justice being present, one where she broke her hand, and both she and the on-again, off-again boyfriend were sent to jail. I had spoken to Sandy earlier the same evening of this fight; she was telling me she was going to put herself and Justice on a bus to head toward where we live, where she would be turning herself in for some theft charges, hoping to be jailed for about a month, and once again requesting that Justice come stay with us. I had agreed that I would pick up Justice at the bus station when they were to arrive the next day. The fight then occurred about 3 am; the local social service agency was contacted, and Sandy immediately told them to call us. Unfortunately, we turn our phones off during the late night and early morning hours, so I didn't know of this turn of events until about 10 the following morning.

When I got the call from Social Services letting me know that Justice had been put into emergency foster care the night before, they asked if I would drive down to Roanoke and pick her up. Although I agreed immediately, in the meantime, the City Attorney decided that the "wheels of government" had begun to churn, and since Justice had now been in foster care for about seven hours, it was too late for us to get her. This started a nine-month court battle to get her to come to our home. Sandy continued to fight, in every court hearing, to have her stay with us, even sending me letters from jail asking us to adopt Justice so that she and Callee could remain together. In the meantime, Justice's birth dad had heard that she was in foster care, and although he didn't really have an interest in raising her, he thought that he could get his dad, Justice's grandfather, to do so. So at first, we were two different "relatives" (the court considers us as relatives since Callee and Justice are birth sisters, and Callee was our daughter) opposing each other for custody.

Justice was able to spend Thanksgiving and Christmas holidays with us; we assumed that she would be home with us permanently by January. Since Justice's grandfather lives close by, we worked a schedule out with him while she was here with us so that she could stay with him for a portion of each holiday time. And as the time drew near for the court hearing in January, I was told that the grandfather was going to just drop his petition for custody, allowing us to have full custody of

Justice, and then to adopt her.

Unfortunately, things did not go as well at the hearing as we had anticipated. The social service agency was reluctant to give over custody at the time because they did not want to have to continue to provide the extra insurance necessary for Justice to have therapy as a victim of domestic violence. Our health insurance is structured so that we cannot have a child covered until adoption papers are drawn up and signed. This left us in a last-minute quandary; Justice had to have health insurance, both from a precautionary standpoint as well as coverage for ongoing therapy. The judge continued the case AGAIN until we could work out something with social services. The city attorney assured us that we could work it out, and Justice would be home in no time.

I was so discouraged; Justice needed to come home with us, but we seemed to be at an impasse with the social service agency. They were not going to help us make sure she had health coverage. In fact, although the agency initially told us at the hearing that they would work with us to make sure Justice could come home, their director changed her mind because she interpreted our lack of ability to provide the insurance as our desire for social services to provide funds to us. This was NOT what we were trying to accomplish, and I felt it was extremely irresponsible for the agency to allow us to have custody of Justice without any way of providing health insurance for her.

God works in ways we don't think of, but His ways are always higher than ours. Justice's grandfather contacted us and asked if we would consider a joint custody arrangement with him, whereby we would have Justice with us, raise her, and he would help us by providing the requisite insurance. This arrangement was the best for her, and for each of us who wanted to be able to make sure she was with us, with her sister, and in a safe and loving home. Sandy wasn't thrilled about the arrangement, as she wanted us to have Justice without the grandfather's assistance, but this was the best way for all of us to be able to provide for her and have her remain in contact with her grandfather and his family. The adoption can now proceed, along with our ability to make sure Justice has full health insurance through our carrier, as she's insured as soon as adoption placement papers are signed.

As I reminded Sandy, sometimes having our children requires a fight, and they are each worth fighting for.

Like Rebekah has experienced, the after-effects of the trauma from the domestic violence can be severe in Justice's life. We have not, as yet, seen intellectual delays with Justice; in fact, she is very bright for her age. However, the most current research indicates that children who have been exposed to domestic violence experience higher levels of anger, aggression, hostility, fear, withdrawal, and poor social relationships. The aggressive behavior we continue to observe with Justice is frustrating; a three-year-old who has no qualms about beating on the older kids whenever she doesn't get her way (or just to annoy them for no reason!) is alarming. She is participating in trauma, art, and play therapy, as well as learning how to live as the youngest in a large family without aggressively attacking her siblings.

The research literature also indicates that children exposed to domestic violence are more likely to experience difficulties in learning and cognitive skills. Justice is precocious for her age, but we are starting her into a homeschooling program, combined with the private preschool that she attends, that will hopefully give her a leg up in case she experiences any cognitive delays later on. We're working with her on beginning letter and phonic sounds so that she will be interested in learning to read early—as a precautionary measure to combat possible struggles in learning later on. We are going to continue to encourage her as she matures to be a strong woman, as girls who are domestic violence victims tend to grow up to become victims as adults. We want to prayerfully and willfully, with careful training, help her and Rebekah both to remember that they are in charge of their own lives, and that God has a plan for them, which doesn't include becoming a victim of any type of violence.

Justice has captured the hearts of everyone here in our family, as well as those who are working with her in preschool and in therapy, despite the violent tendancies. She loves life, and is excited to be in a large family where there is always someone who will engage with her either outside with the animals, the bikes, or something involving a ball (soccer, volleyball, or basketball), or inside the playroom working on their made-up gymnastics or dance routines. She's my Velcro child, hanging on for dear life when she's dropped off at school, in children's church on Sundays, or in her own gymnastics class. But she's friendly and outgoing once she leaves my side, and I know God has blessed us so much with finally having her home.

Justice (age 4) says: *I like having a mom and dad. I like having lots of sisters and a brother to play with, and my own mini donkey named Buddy.*

IN THE NICK OF TIME

Again, as we are going to publication, we have been blessed with yet another addition to our family. Nichole was in foster care with our best friends, beginning at the age of 15. She stayed with us off and on when our friends traveled out of the country, and to babysit. We grew close to her, and when things didn't work out for her at our friends' home, we offered Social Services to take her into our home through foster care.

With no clear reason, the agency refused to allow Nichole to live with us, although we were the only other family that she knew well and was comfortable with. Instead, they moved her to an out of the way country home, in hopes that she would find it difficult to run away. Essentially, they were setting her up for failure. She wanted to live with us, she was 17, and had two and a half more years of high school. When the agency refused our offer and her pleading, without any explanation to either of us, she bolted. The agency then, in an attempt to "get her off of their hands" went to court and let the judge know that her birth family was now appropriate and capable of parenting her, releasing her to them. Sadly, the entire court proceeding was a farce, as Nichole's mother was still living with the boyfriend who had physically abused Nichole. Furthermore, Nichole had not gone to school for years while supposedly under her mother's care, and there was no indication that she would do so this time.

Nichole was immediately put in the position of fending for herself, in much the same way as she and her two older sisters had for most of their lives. Although only a sophomore in high school, she had nowhere to live, and therefore no school to go to, or any form of transportation. We continued to try to contact her, until I finally realized we had a phone number that was no longer assigned to her, and we lost touch. She did the couch hopping thing for a few years, eventually landing in jail for a DUI, having never gotten a driver's license.

I began corresponding with Nichole while she was in jail, as it was the first time in two years that I knew where she was and how to contact her. She wrote me to let me know what was going on with her. When I went to visit her in the jail, she told me that I was the only one who had ever come to see her there (this was actually her second stint in jail – this time for six weeks, as she had no one to bail her out).

One thing I've learned about our justice system is that the poor are the ones who suffer the most from it – they do not have the means to make bail, they do not have the funds for court imposed finds or court imposed programs, so they end up back in jail since they can't afford the fees. This is exactly what had happened to Nichole – she was sentenced to a state drinking and driving program, but when she went to sign up for it, she was told she had to pay $400, which she didn't have. So, not being in compliance, she was put back into jail.

Here's the catch: in Virginia, if you are sentenced to this type of alcohol/driving program, you have to pay it up front. But if you end up going back to jail because you're unable to pay, the second time, they will allow you to make payment arrangements. So basically, indigent people are automatically going to have to serve more time in jail because they don't have the funds up front the first time to pay for the programs. Doesn't make sense to me, nor to the other attorneys I've worked with, and I'm sure this is why so many people get angry with "the system" because of the way it seems to prey on the poor.

Nichole's beginnings were rough, as is the case with most of our children. She was neglected by an alcoholic mother and drug addicted father. She doesn't remember a time when her parents (still currently married after about 25 years, but not living together for at least the last 19 or 20 years) were together unless it was when they were fighting and breaking up. She remembers moving "all the time" because they were constantly being evicted. She remembers rarely having electricity wherever they were living, and numerous times with no running water.

Nichole states there was a brief time she remembers living with her dad, but it was in a van. She says that she, her mother, and her two sisters lived in a van, a car, or shelters numerous times, moved in with her grandmother occasionally, or lived with her mother's various boyfriends. During most of this time period, she didn't go to school. She was propositioned to have sex with one of her mom's boyfriends that they were forced to live with; she thinks she was about twelve or thirteen. Her sisters have told her that the three of them were in foster care when they were little, but she doesn't remember it.

From about age twelve, Nichole didn't go to school at all. She describes her childhood as raising herself, or her sisters pitching in to raise her. She smoked her first cigarette at age six, given to her by her older sister. She drank her first beer at age twelve, also procured by her sister, and slowly became an alcoholic. At age thirteen, while at a party, her beer was drugged and she was raped. When she told her mother the next day, all hell broke loose – her mom called Nichole a slut and said she had it coming to her.

Nichole lived with various family friends from about age twelve to age fifteen. During a brief time trying to live again with her mother and the most current boyfriend, "Ron" pulled her hair out, smashed her to the ground, and kicked her repeatedly. She escaped to a friend's house, and Social Services were called. This landed Nichole in foster care, at our friend's home, which was when we first met her.

Because Nichole had been out of school for so long, the social worker and the public school system were unsure as to what grade to place her in. At fifteen, she should have been either a freshman or a sophomore in high school, but was far behind her peers due to her lack of school attendance. The decision was finally made to put her into an alternative school for middle school students as an eighth grader.

Unfortunately, the alternative school is usually a placement for children with behavioral problems. So anytime there was a discrepancy at school, it was assumed that Nichole had an attitude, or was a behavior problem, rather than the teachers and staff attempting to resolve it as they would in a regular school setting. It was a miserable school experience for Nichole; our friends that she lived with constantly agonized over a better school setting for her. At the end of her eighth grade year, although she hadn't caught up the other students, it was determined she should be placed at the local high school with special education help. By the end of her sophomore year, when she was kicked out of foster care, she had completely caught up to her peers, and was on the honor role.

During high school, the drinking problem Nichole had became more apparent. She was partying with friends from school, and drinking every day, sometimes even before school. Our friends were doing their best to help her, but a young teenage alcoholic is difficult to deal with, and she wasn't admitting to herself that she had a problem (although our friends tried to tell her she did). For a brief time Nichole was dancing and modeling, so she was able to curtail the drinking a bit, but not enough to stop completely. As she describes it now, she knows she was self-medicating to get rid of the pain she refused to acknowledge, dealing with the struggles she had always felt in raising herself, not feeling that she was truly cared for and cherished. Although she was loved by our friends (and by us as well), she couldn't feel it or understand it.

As much as our friends, Nichole's foster parents, were trying to get help for her and asking the social service agency to help, they were completely ignored by the agency. Eventually, in a completely irrational staging of a legal fiction (claiming Nichole's birth mother and boyfriend were now able and willing to care for her, although they were not), the agency convinced the judge to release Nichole from foster care. This plunged her into an adult world that she was not prepared to live in, having to completely fend for herself, unable to enroll herself into school, and thus resigning her to homelessness and continued alcoholism. She spiraled out of control, was drinking and driving (without a license) which landed her in jail.

Her tragedy became an incredible blessing for her and for us as we reconnected, showed her how much she has been loved and wanted all this time, even when we lost touch with her (and never stopped praying for her). I can honestly say that although I would never wish anyone to go to jail, this has been a major turning point in Nichole's life that God has used to show her how much He loves her and what an incredible plan He has for her life.

Nichole says: *I love being a part of the Steele family because I finally have stability and all of the love I could ever ask for. I also feel I have a brand new start to life, and I love having so many brothers and sisters! Having two parents that I know will never give up on me or tell me I can't be what I want to be is amazing.*

A DAY IN THE LIFE

So what is it like to be the parents of a large family? Well, we have an added advantage, if you want to call it that, of our older children choosing to be in a large family. They know what they are getting into before they are actually adopted, whereas the younger ones, while they get excited about another new sibling, don't have as much of a choice since they've been here since they were babies or toddlers.

Our days are like many of yours, just with more organization perhaps. The youngest four children are usually the first up—early even when we'd like to sleep in over weekends and holidays. On schooldays, they head downstairs to hang out with Dad, who is up every morning by 5 AM. Alan makes breakfast for them, usually either cereal or something with bacon (eggs or an egg and bacon sandwich) after they watch the news with him for awhile.

Because Jake and Callee are in special education classes in the public schools, their buses arrive after I've left to take the kids to private school, so Alan generally remains home until their buses arrive at the driveway of our ranch to pick them up.

I'm up by 6 am, I shower, and then gather everyone's clothes for the morning, making sure the five little ones have their teeth brushed, hair neat or brushed (Tawnee, Taylor, Justice, and Callee have braids, so theirs is redone about every two weeks). Everyone has their own backpack and lunchbox, shoes on (yes, we have left the house with Jake only in socks) and coats or jackets except in warmer weather.

As I'm getting the little ones together, the older girls are slowly struggling out of bed, usually running for the school bus just as it arrives in front of our house. At one time we had eight kids in six different schools, so there was a lot of scurrying in different directions in the mornings; fortunately we're now down to 3 different schools for 7 kids!

I get by on doing two loads of laundry a day, so I usually start one just before we leave for school. I have to rush back after the school run to feed all of the animals, and I often run errands for our business after I drop the kids off, and try to get another load of laundry done in the morning, if possible. Alan and I both work from home, but he is gone most of the day. I usually have to take one of the kids (or more) either to counseling, doctor's appointments, the dentist, or the orthodontist a couple of days during the week, with morning court appearances once or twice every week.

Thankfully, Alan's schedule is flexible, so one or both of us are available by the time the kids get out of school around 2:45 each day for driving to therapy, music lessons, or sports. The kids are supposed to get their homework done right after school and read their Bibles so that they can play, practice music lessons, ride the horses, go to sports practice, or just chill with a book.

Aimee and Rebekah have sports practice after school as well as later in the evenings (volleyball, soccer, and basketball, depending on the season); the younger girls have gymnastics and soccer; Jake plays soccer as well. We generally don't allow television during the week before or after school, unless there's a movie we all watch together.

We are firm believers that Americans have too much "stuff", particularly new stuff. If it can be obtained used, we get it used. That goes for cars, house, bikes, often clothes, and sometimes toys. We love Craigslist and Ebay for the special, high-priced birthday and Christmas gifts like hand-held games and American Girl dolls. We try to get bikes, scooters, skates, skateboards, and any other mode of transportation, used if possible. We love yard sales. At a recent one we found clothes and shoes for the girls that had never been worn, and even a saddle we needed for one of the horses.

We don't use credit cards, and pay cash for everything, attempting to teach our children that if you don't have the money for something, you don't get to buy it until you do. There are several upscale teen and children's resale shops in our area, as well as a terrific thrift store, where we can pick up gently used clothes, shoes (particularly for the older girls and myself, who are shoe fiends) and sometimes toys for a fraction of the cost of new. I am also a firm believer that children need a library of books, so in addition to several trips to the library each week (for myself as well as the kids), the special books that we need to have added to our home library we get from Half.com.

Since Alan used to own grocery stores and markets, he has always enjoyed going to the grocery store (my mother urged me to marry him for that reason—she hates grocery shopping). So he goes, usually taking at least one of the kids in tow, at least once every other day, sometimes once a day. He also likes to be the one to make dinner, so we can eat when he wants and what he wants. Tawnee and Callee both have food issues related to their Reactive Attachment Disorder (RAD), so they are often hovering around Alan and the kitchen as dinner is being made. They like to "help," which often means making sure they are not too close to the stove for my comfort. Tawnee has been an interested food preparer since she was a toddler, and it's become a habit. (Her career goal is to be a "cooker.") Callee often feels the need to call Dad during the afternoon if he's not home from work before she gets home from school. She wants to find out what we're having for dinner, and to instruct him that she wants hamburgers and French fries.

One of the after-affects of RAD for both of our younger girls is their uncertainty that their need for food will be satisfied. They were often hungry during their nomadic times with their birth moms before foster care. Since they never attached to an adult who would meet their needs, there remains this residual feeling deep inside them, even though they have both been provided with three meals a day, every day, since they were little (15 months for Tawnee, from the time she came to us, and three years old for Callee, at the time she entered her foster home). They often resemble little vultures or baby birds, ready to pounce when they hear the refrigerator or the pantry door open.

Tawnee, in particular, seems to carry deeply rooted fears. She is always interested to the point of obsession as to what each child has in their lunchbox, the amount of food each person has for dinner, and will often finish two or three other children's dinners after bolting down her own. Alan is constantly reminding her, "We have more, you don't have to worry about eating fast. You'll get second portions." She is tall and skinny, so we don't worry about her weight, at least for now. I often pray that God will keep her from any eating disorders as she grows older.

Dinnertime is the one time of the day when the entire family is together. We try, as much as possible, to schedule dinner around any sports practices, therapies, and music lessons. Our dinner table is often crowded when the older kids and their spouses are home, or someone has a friend over, but we make it work. Alan is used to cooking for a tribe of people, so one or two more are always welcome. We eat buffet style, with everyone serving themselves from the kitchen, and then eating together after prayers in the dining room.

We rarely eat out unless it's a special occasion, like a birthday. Each child is allowed to pick where they would like the family to eat out on their birthday (except a popular kid arcade-and-pizza joint, a place that drives both Alan and I insane). The newest fad is for the kids to pick a breakfast place for their birthday to go to with just Dad, and we try to take at least one kid out per week for Mom or Dad alone time for a soda or an ice cream treat.

Everyone helps set the table and then clears afterward so that I can do dishes (only fair, since Alan cooks) with the older girls. We often watch a movie together after dinner if there are no other activities we are driving kids to—during soccer season, one of us is at a soccer practice almost every night of the week, as we have between five and six kids playing soccer each fall or spring. Oftentimes one of the girls is getting their hair braided, so they get to pick the movie, since they have to be the "captive audience" while getting their hair done. Aimee, Taylor, and Tawnee are on the local speed skating team, skating with inline skates in an indoor rink, and they practice early on Saturday mornings and after dinner one night a week.

Being in a big family means that everyone has to help—the older ones help with the younger ones; each child is responsible for picking up after themselves, and I spend time redirecting the kids to be responsible for their own stuff.

Having animals is another way for the kids to learn responsibility. It's also therapeutic. We have a rabbit, a dog named JoJo, a cat, four horses, five alpacas, three llamas, two miniature horses, a miniature donkey and a mini pot bellied pig named Charlotte. Callee, Tawnee, and Jake take turns feeding the dog and helping to care for the horses, llamas, alpacas with the older girls.

I keep a journal for each child. I didn't start writing in individual journals for them until Kara was fourteen, when I started hers and began Aimee's. So Kevin and Brendan did not get the advantage of having one, and reading what I write about them—I try to write them letters and let them know how proud I am of them. I gave Kara's journal to her when she moved out after college; I save the other journals for each child for when they marry. I don't write in them every day, just on special days in their lives and when I feel like it. Each child knows I write in a journal for them, and even though I don't let them read theirs now, it gives them a sense of safety and well-being. "Mom writes about me to show how much they love me."

We recently moved out to the country to a small ranch with a six-bedroom home so that we could have a larger home and a place for the animals. Our animals are all rescues, and we are working a therapeutic riding program on our ranch now for kids with all kinds of challenges and disabilities. The kids complain about helping with the animals, but I know they enjoy it, because they brag about living in the country to their friends when they think we're not listening.

So the starfish story is our story. We will keep on tossing those starfish back into God's ocean of love.

We never know what will happen to each starfish once it's tossed back in, but we want to make sure each of our starfish is surrounded by our own sea of love as well as God's. We don't know how many more starfish God will lay at our feet, just that we need to be prepared to work with each of them with their own special needs before they are tossed back into that ocean, ready for God to do His work in their lives. There's always more waves to ride on the ocean God sets before us, and always more chapters to be written in the stories of our children's lives.

WHERE THEY ARE NOW?

Many people have asked about our oldest three children, who are mentioned in this book, but do not have their complete stories told. We shared custody of Brendan and Kara with their birth mom, and had full custody of Kevin throughout most of their growing-up years. Brendan, now 34, is a photographer with his own gallery and works in commercial fishing in Alaska. He has an amazing talent as an art photographer.

Kevin, age 31, has been in the Army for over 11 years and is on his second tour in Afghanistan. He is stationed near our home for the first time since he began his Army career, so we are enjoying seeing him for weekends and longer stays. He traveled down to South Carolina for his sister Evelyn's boot camp graduation on his first day of leave after his arrival from his first Afghanistan tour. This was highly meaningful for her, and of course, a blast for us after being away from him for so long. It is much better for my heart to have him back in the country and away from a danger zone, so I'll be glad when this tour is over. It's also nice for both of them to be living at the same base, although they don't get to see each other very much.

Kara started working with Southwest Airlines at age 18 after graduating from high school and visiting our relatives in Europe for a couple of months. She is still with Southwest now at age 27, married to a wonderful Army guy named, appropriately, Ryan Steele (how nice that she didn't have to change her last name) and we have two beautiful granddaughters: Courtney, age seven , and Caitlin, almost three.

Although some people find it a little strange that our youngest daughter, Taylor, has a niece only a year younger than her, we enjoy having grandkids as well as young kids.

As for Alan and myself, God continues to work in our lives through the children we are asked to take in as a part of our family.

We never know how our lives and our family will change, but there's always more room at the dinner table.

Kevin and Alan Steele

Kevin says: *"I like having a lot of younger siblings, and enjoy getting to see them and getting to know them whenever I can."*

AFTERWORD – ONLY THE BEGINNING

Our job in this life is to point others toward Jesus Christ, and show the world how much God loves them by bringing us His Son to take our place in the judgment of our sins. When I hear people say to me, "Oh, you and your husband are amazing, saving these children," I stop them. I have to tell them that Alan and I are the ones to be saved from our complacency, from what would have been an easier life after raising three kids and then doing what our friends do. They have much more leisure time, they travel more, take more vacations, and they are able to use their hard-earned money on themselves. Our money is used for ever-growing children—clothes, soccer fees and more cleats for seven kids, speed skating lessons for five, basketball uniforms, swim team fees, and child care when we take a small vacation together. But we are the ones who are saved, who are blessed.

Our older children are blessed as younger siblings need their good examples and guidance (even though they don't always look upon it as a blessing). Our parents and our own siblings are blessed by having more grandchildren, nieces, and nephews. And we are blessed by having a loving God. We are blessed by showing each of our children that God loves them, so that they can in turn share that love with the rest of the world. They learn that though they have disabilities, God has given them gifts and abilities to share. No one is a perfect parent, or a perfect kid, but God uses us anyway.

It wouldn't be fair if I didn't let each of you know that YOU can make a difference in a child's life. In our country alone, there are almost half a million kids that are waiting for parents. In almost all cases, it doesn't cost anything to adopt the waiting children in this country, and sometimes there is a stipend to help with raising a child. And if you think you are too old, or don't have enough money, or don't have a large home, you don't need any of those things. You only need a heart open to what God can do, and the willingness for Him to use you in the life of a child. If it is not possible for you to adopt, you can still be used to help out those who are called to change these children's lives. Offer to baby-sit, or pick up clothes for adopted children, or make a meal for the adoptive family. Everyone can be used to make a difference in the lives of the fatherless.

I was recently shopping at a local boutique's huge 75-80 percent off sale. After describing a few of my daughters to the owner and her sales clerks, the owner came in with a huge bag of clothes in different sizes from the store that she wanted to "give" to my daughters. This woman was used by God in a way she never expected, and certainly I never did either. At another recent shopping excursion to a teen resale shop, someone recognized us from a television show that had aired on us. She said God had touched her heart about our family, and she wanted to give us her shopping coupon to this particular store that she was just getting ready to use for herself—it gave us half off of all of our summer clothing purchases! During the missions trip that Alan and

I took to Ethiopia, a friend agreed to stay at our home with our children entirely for free, as an offering to the Lord.

There are children all over our nation who pray each night that God will bring them a family. God works through His children, through you and I, to make the prayers of the fatherless come to pass. You and I are His hands and feet, His ears and eyes, His love to the children in a dying world that are crying out to be loved and cherished, just like He has loved and cherished us.

Just as this book is headed to the publisher, we got a call from the same local agency that our daughters Tawnee and Taylor were adopted from, asking if we would be willing to come to court to take custody of their first cousin, Jamal. All of his natural siblings were adopted out before he was born; his birth mom "slipped under the wire" with her pregnancy with him, and once it was reported to Social Services that he had been born and was living with her, they decided they were going to give her one last chance to keep her child. We have continued to visit with Jamal and with his grandmothers since our girls were adopted, and knew he was in potential danger for his physical safety, but felt there was little that we could do other than report what we personally observed to Social Services.

Unfortunately, Jamal has been the one to suffer by Social Service's reluctance to take charge and remove him from her care. He is now six; he was molested as an infant, and physically abused. He has endured much in the way of witnessing, and being in the middle of, domestic violence in a never-ending battle between his mom, his grandmother, and the grandmother's boy-friend, not to mention the various unsavory boyfriends of his mom. He has lived in a small two-bedroom apartment with as many as fifteen other people, most of them complete strangers. He has been sleeping in a bed with the man who was accused of molesting him.

Several months ago, Social Services finally stepped in and removed him from his mother's care, putting him with his birth father, who lived nearby but had never been involved in his care before, only having weekly visits. Sadly, although the father said he was going to care for Jamal himself, he immediately put him back into the grandmother's care, which resulted in his same living situation—the domestic violence, the physical abuse, and having to live and sleep with his al-leged abuser from his infanthood. The father had been made aware of the dangerous living situation his son was in over the last six years, but was either unwill-ing to believe it, or unwilling to do anything to make a change for him.

Jamal was taken to the emergency room last week with a high fever, and the nurse asked him where he had gotten the huge goose-egg bump and scratch on his head. He responded, "My mom hit me," and of course, the medical professionals had to report it. Finally, the Social Service agency decided to remove him from his birth family, which is the first act of safety they have done since he was born six years ago.

They have now requested that we take custody of him, and we have filed a petition with the court. The decision will be made within the next few weeks, allowing us to add to our family yet again, and giving us the blessing of another boy.

Jake is excited to be able to have a roommate and, finally, someone else with testosterone who will live here permanently (Kevin and our sons-in-law visit, but don't stay long enough for Jake's desires)! God's blessings are never-ending, and living a life submitted to Him, while never easy, is never dull.

SCRIPTURES FOR REFERENCE

*Religion that God our Father accepts as
pure and faultless is this: to look after orphans
and widows in their distress and to keep oneself
from being polluted by the world.*
JAMES 1:27

*Do not take advantage of a widow or an orphan.
If you do and they cry out to me, I will certainly
hear their cry.*
EXODUS 22:22, 23

*Defend the cause of the weak and the fatherless;
maintain the rights of the poor and oppressed.*
PSALM 82:3

*Learn to do right. Seek justice, encourage the op-
pressed. Defend the cause of the fatherless,
plead the case of the widow.*
ISAIAH 1:17

*You hear, O Lord, the desire of the afflicted; you
encourage them, and you listen to their cry, defending
the fatherless and the oppressed, in order that man,
who is of the earth, may terrify no more.*
PSALM 10:17, 18

ACKNOWLEDGEMENTS

I would like to thank those people kind and patient enough to make this book a reality: my publisher, Larry Carpenter of Carpenter's Son's Publishing; designer, Suzanne Lawing; editor, Robert Irvin; marketing consultant, Lorraine Bosse'-Smith with Concept One; and my mom, Margi Wynn, artist extraordinaire, for the cover design. This book was also made possible by the encouragement of Pastor Mike Macintosh, of Horizon Christian Fellowship in San Diego; Pastor Norlyn Kent, of Horizon South Bay in San Diego; Colleen Barrett, President Emeritus of Southwest Airlines, as well as Lynne Kohm, a dear friend, fellow attorney and writer. Thanks be to God, who makes all things possible through faith in His Son!